ACE YOUR MEDICAL SCHOOL INTERVIEW

INCLUDES MULTIPLE MINI INTERVIEWS MMI FOR MEDICAL SCHOOL

BY DR PETER GRIFFITHS

Contents

Dr Peter Griffiths qualified as a doctor from St. George's University of London in 2009 where he was a multi-award winning graduate. He has helped many hundreds of people gain entry to medical school around the world both with this book and also with his extremely popular book "Griffiths Gamsat Review" which helps students prepare for the GAMSAT – Graduate Medical School Admissions Test. More information about his GAMSAT preparation materials for candidates required to sit this test for entry to medical school can be found on his website at –

www.gamsatreview.com

"To be a great champion, you must believe that you are the best. If you're not, pretend you are."
- Muhammad Ali

Why You Need This Book

At some stage you may have been given the interview advice "Just be yourself" or "The interviewers just want to get to know you as a person".

Unfortunately unless you are already very well prepared indeed for your medical school interview, this advice is likely to lead you to interview failure.

What exactly does "be yourself" mean? Does it mean you should talk to the interviewers as you talk to your friends in the pub? No, of course not. The fact of the matter is that we all project different personas or aspects of our personality in different situations.

This does not mean we are being false or "not being ourselves", it is just a part of normal human and social interaction.

The aim of this book is not to persuade you to be somebody you are not. Its purpose is to help you realise your full potential and show you how you can project your best possible characteristics in the interview.

And that is exactly what the interviewers want to see, your best possible characteristics, for no interviewer is hoping that a candidate will do badly when they walk through the door.

Remember there is intense competition for medical school places and you can be sure that a lot of the candidates you are competing against will be taking the interview very seriously. They will be making a lot of effort researching and rehearsing their answers.

If you want to maximise your own chances of success, then you will have to do the same. This book is an aid to help you do that. By having all the information you need in one place, this book will save you a lot of time. However you will still need to put the effort in to prepare yourself.

Good luck!

How To Use This Book

This book provides a lot of the typical questions you will be asked in your medical school interview. Suggested answers are provided to many of them.

The purpose of the suggested answers is NOT for you to learn them and repeat parrot fashion in your interview!

The purpose of the suggested answers is to show you the style of a good answer and to make you aware of important issues or areas which the med schools may be looking for in your answers.

By all means use the answers given in this book as the basis for your own answers if you feel they are appropriate to you. However, adapt them to your own specific circumstances and above all put them in your own words.

If you try to use language or words in your answers which you do not normally use then you will just end up sounding contrived and rehearsed. Practice your answers so that you feel comfortable saying them in your own style.

Nevertheless, having said the above, there is also a lot of useful factual information in this book. For example, the qualities of a good doctor as given by the GMC, information about PBL, historical achievements in medicine, ethical issues etc. etc.

This information is provided for your convenience so feel free to memorise it exactly as it appears here and use it in your answers.

Four Things To Do
Before Your Interview

1. Research the med school

Find out all you can about the med school where you have been offered the interview. There are two reasons to do this. Firstly because you may be asked questions such as "Why did you apply to this school?" or "What interests you about the course here?" and you will look decidedly silly if you don't have an answer.

Secondly, at the end of the interview you may be asked if you have any questions to ask the interviewers. You really don't want to ask a question to which the answer is easily found on the university website. This will just make you look lazy and like you really didn't have much interest in that med school in the first place.

Try to access as many different sources of information about the med school as you can. Look at their website, look at the hard copy of their prospectus (which often contains different information to that found on the website). Re-read carefully any letters or information they have sent you during the application process as these may also contain useful information.

2. Research the interview

You are trying to discover two things, firstly, what is the format of the interview? Will you be interviewed by a single person or a panel? Will the interview be very formal and have you sitting in a chair in front of a row of interviewers behind desks or will it be a more informal arrangement around a coffee table? Will there be any kind of case study you will have to prepare/comment on?

You will probably have been told all this by the med school at the time they offered you your interview, but if not try and find out. Don't be afraid to ring the med school directly to find out if necessary, they are usually quite helpful.

Secondly, can you find any clues as to the kinds of questions you may be asked? It is very unlikely that you will find exact questions but many med schools are surprisingly forthcoming on their web sites etc. about the general topics or areas that questions may cover. If you apply to St. George's University of London for example it should come as no surprise to you in the interview if you are asked questions about the importance of research since this is emphasised on the St. George's web site.

3. Research yourself

One of the most frequent mistakes that candidates in interviews make is not being able to talk sufficiently convincingly about themselves. Scrutinise your personal statement that you made on your application form carefully. Be prepared to elaborate on all aspects of it. For every personal achievement, activity or hobby you have mentioned, be prepared to answer the following questions:

- Why did you do it?

- What skills/qualities did it require?

- What are the good and bad things about it?

- What have you learnt from it?

- Would you do anything differently with the benefit of hindsight?

4. Do mock interviews

If you are lucky enough to have been offered several interviews from different med schools then you will probably find that your interview technique improves from the first to the last. Practice makes perfect. However you cannot afford to waste the first interview or two as "practice" interviews and hope that your technique will be sufficiently developed for the third or fourth. You need to have already done some practice interviews before your first interview so you can hit the ground running.

Your school or university will most likely have someone who can give you mock interviews. If not try and get a friend or family member to do it for you.

Use the research you have done previously to try and model your mock interviews on the same format as your real interviews i.e. if it is a panel interview try and get more than one person in the mock interview to be asking questions, or if there is a case study, try and include one in your mock interview too.

You should be trying to achieve the following goals in your mock interviews:

• Clarifying your answers in your own mind

You may look at a potential interview question and think you know the answer, maybe it's so obvious you don't even need to think about how you will word your reply. Wrong!! There is a big difference between having an answer in your head and saying it out loud.

You may need to practice several times before you can get the phrasing just right and sound fluid and natural without fumbling for words or saying "errmm". You wouldn't try to give a speech without practising it out loud at least once would you? Well interview answers are just the same, you need to say them out loud to really see how your answers sound.

• Practising your body language

If you can, videotape your interview, not only will you hear exactly how you sound afterwards but you will be able to see how you look as well. What kind of expression do you have on your face? Do you look confident or just terrified? Are you sitting upright or slouching etc?

If you don't have access to a video recorder then get your mock "interviewer" to take notes on your body language as well as your answers.

• Overcoming your nerves

You won't feel as nervous in a mock interview as you will in the real thing, but I guarantee that when you get to the real thing the mere fact that you have done some mock interviews will make you feel less nervous.

Not only will you know what to expect but as you will have practised your answers several times already you will be feeling much more confident.

Remember that nervousness is one of the main reasons candidates do badly at interview. Nerves freeze up your mind and prevent you from thinking quickly or getting your words out properly. So anything you can do to feel less nervous is important.

After each mock interview make sure you get

constructive criticism from the person interviewing you and use their comments to refine your answers and then practice them again.

INSIDER DEALING

It may be illegal in the world of finance, but when it comes to interviews there's no reason not to get any advantage you can. If possible speak to students who are already studying at the med schools where you have interviews.

In many cases their tutors and lecturers may be the people who will be interviewing you. They will probably have a much better understanding of the ethos and culture of each individual med school and what are the particular issues you are likely to be asked about at interview. They may also be able to give you tips from their own interview experience

If you don't know any current students perhaps your school or university can put you in touch with past pupils who are now studying at the medical schools you have applied to. Ask your careers adviser or alumni office for help.

Dress for Success

When I went for some of my medical school interviews I was shocked by what some of the other candidates felt was appropriate dress for an interview. Men wearing jumpers instead of suits and women wearing frumpy dresses that looked like something they would go to the supermarket in.

Now maybe you think that people shouldn't be judged on their appearance. Maybe you think that in your interview you should be judged on what you say rather than what you wear. Maybe I even agree with you. But the fact of the matter is no-one cares what we think. The reality of the situation is that appearance counts.

Research has shown conclusively that in job interviews, physical appearance is one of the main determining factors (if not the determining factor) as to who will be the successful candidate. And furthermore interviewers reach their opinions about candidates within the first minute of meeting them.

Now medical school interviews are probably more structured than a typical job interview, so the situation MAY not be exactly the same. Nevertheless the interviewer is likely to form a very quick initial impression of you based almost entirely on your appearance and this may influence them either consciously or unconsciously in terms of how they score your answers.

You only get one chance to make a good first impression, so DON'T take any chances. Think conservative in your dress, and always remember that too formal is better than too casual. Anything trendy or "the latest style" is probably not appropriate. If in doubt, leave it out of your interview wardrobe.

The following tips will stand you in good stead:

For men

- A two piece business suit in dark blue or dark grey

- A long sleeved shirt in plain white or pale blue

- A button up cuff on the shirt is fine. Cufflinks are not necessary and if you do not normally wear them they are only likely to make you feel more self- conscious.

- A silk tie, either plain or with a conservative pattern. A light colour such as pale yellow, pink or light blue can nicely offset the dark colour of the suit, however avoid anything bright or garish and avoid red

- Black socks

- Black lace up shoes (no brown shoes)

- No more than one ring on each hand

- Neat, well trimmed hair

- Clean trimmed fingernails

- Minimal after-shave

- Avoid putting bulky items into pockets, which make them bulge, or too many coins which can jingle.

- No beards or moustaches (sorry if you have them but they are undoubtedly a negative in interviews especially with female interviewers)

- Definitely no earrings or piercings

For women

- A dark colour suit with a jacket and skirt or trousers, no dresses. I do not recommend black suits for men since it can make them look like they are going to a funeral, however the extra gravitas that black imparts can suit women and make them seem more businesslike.

- A conservative white or pastel blouse

- Shoes with conservative heels

- Neat well styled hair

- Discrete make-up

- Clear or pale nail varnish, no bright colours

- No more than two rings per hand

- One pair of earrings only

- No piercings

- Minimal perfume

- A briefcase or portfolio case is preferable to carrying a purse or handbag

Finally bear in mind that many people, particularly of the older generation, pay particular attention to a persons' shoes. It is a common belief that someone who doesn't pay attention to their shoes doesn't pay attention to details. So ensure that your shoes are clean and well polished.

The Waiting Game

It goes without saying that you should arrive for your interview with plenty of time to spare. Make use of this spare time to visit the toilet and comb your hair if necessary and then enter the waiting area and make yourself known to the secretary/administrator.

Assess the layout of the waiting area and try to sit in a chair where you can see the interviewers entering the room and make eye contact easily. Sit down, relax and compose your thoughts.

In my experience, if there are any other candidates waiting they will rarely try and talk to you. If anyone does attempt to engage you in conversation reply with one-word answers and hopefully they will get the message and leave you alone. Now is not the time to become distracted.

Take out your personal statement and any interview notes you have prepared for a final review. Mentally rehearse your answers to standard questions and visualise yourself smiling and confident in the interview.

If necessary practice any relaxation techniques you have to get rid of any pre interview jitters (some simple techniques will be explained later).

Don't drink coffee before the interview as the caffeine will just make you more nervous but bring some bottled water to sip so your mouth doesn't get dry.

The Initial Rapport Technique

As mentioned above you should try and choose a seat from where you can easily see and make eye contact with anyone who enters the room. Stay alert and whenever someone enters look up, make eye contact and give a warm smile.

You may end up smiling at a few people who are not your interviewer, but sooner or later it will be your interviewer who enters and their first impression of you will be of an alert, open and friendly person. This will greatly help you to establish a good initial rapport with your interviewer.

The Handshake

Eventually your name will be called and the interviewer will approach you. As before smile warmly and rise calmly to your feet (don't jump up like a startled rabbit). After identifying yourself the interviewer will probably extend his hand to shake yours. If not, do not be afraid to initiate the handshake yourself.

If you tend to have cold hands try sitting on your right hand for a few minutes while waiting to warm it up so you are not shaking hands with a cold clammy hand.

If you are nervous and think your palm is sweating a bit, discretely wipe it on your trousers or the chair before the interviewer approaches you. There is nothing worse than shaking a damp hand. (Tip: If you sweat a lot try rubbing some talcum powder into your hand before leaving for the interview.)

Let the strength of your grip be guided by the interviewer. If he/she has a strong grip, then return the same grip and shake hands firmly. If they have a weaker grip then adjust your grip to the same strength as them.

THE LONG WALK

After the introductions you will then be guided towards the interview room. This may be only next door or it may be some distance away. If it seems that you have a little walk to get to the room do not simply follow the interviewer in silence. Now is the perfect opportunity to continue building your initial rapport.

If your interviewer is pleasant they may save you the effort here by making small talk such as asking you if you had a good journey. If not you will have to do some work yourself.

Take the opportunity to ask a neutral conversational question. You will need to think a little while you are waiting about what you will ask here.

For example if the university building seems very old or have interesting architecture you could make a comment along the lines of "This is quite a historical building isn't it, do you know when it was built?"

Or if you have seen some interesting news about the university on their web site you could ask about that, e.g. "I see that your medical school came in the top three of the Guardian survey of medical schools recently, you must all be very pleased"

Don't worry if you feel your question or comment is boring or inane. Its only purpose here is to emphasise to the interviewer that you are a normal person capable of normal social interactions and to set up a friendly atmosphere before you get into the interview room.

On entering the interview room you may find another two or three people waiting for you if it is a panel interview.

On entering smile warmly again and briefly look round and quickly make eye contact with everyone. Then say hello to the other interviewers individually and shake hands with each.

DIRTY TRICKS

You should be aware that if you are unlucky, some interviewers may use some dirty tricks just to see how you will respond when under stress.

A common technique is to immediately pose an odd or unnecessarily aggressive question. For example in one interview I had, as soon as I had sat down, one of the interviewers virtually shouted at me "So, are you from Timbuctoo?" I stayed calm and said "Sorry, I'm not sure what you mean exactly?" he then smiled and said, "I was just asking if you had to come far to get here?"

Another technique is to keep asking "Anything else?" after you have answered a question. Sometimes this may be of use to you as it provides you with further opportunities to develop your answer or demonstrate further knowledge.

However if you feel you have fully answered a question and genuinely cannot add anything further do not be afraid to say, "No I think I've answered the question as fully as I can". Avoid the temptation to ask if you have missed anything important out or say weakly "I can't think of anything else" as this will just make you appear unsure of yourself.

Body Language

Everyone nowadays is aware of the importance of body language. Your non-verbal communication will say far more about you than the words which come out of your mouth and play a huge role in the impression that the interviewers form about you.

It is vital therefore that you are aware of how you look, your posture, your facial expression and your hand and body movements and gestures.

Unfortunately, because of the widespread knowledge of body language nowadays, many people believe themselves to be experts and that they can tell all about you on the basis of some minor twitch. Did you touch your nose while you were talking? Then you must have been lying (not that you just had an itch). Did you at any point cross your arms? Then of course you are defensive and untrusting (not just feeling a bit cold).

To avoid falling into someone else's stereotype just be aware of the common body signals which can be perceived as indicative of negative traits and try to consciously emphasise those that are associated with positive traits.

Here are some important areas to be aware of:

Eye contact

When someone is nervous it can often be difficult

for them to maintain good eye contact with the person they are talking to. And probably during the interview you will be a little nervous so be aware this is a problem you may have.

If someone doesn't make eye contact while speaking it can make the listener feel uncomfortable too and inhibit a natural and relaxed flow of conversation.

Also not making eye contact, or continually looking up or down can also be perceived as signals that you are not telling the truth or are untrustworthy.

Therefore make a conscious effort to maintain steady and confident eye contact with the interviewer (but don't stare fixedly like a psychopath) both when you are speaking and when they are speaking to you. If you have more than one interviewer, during your answers remember to turn your head and make eye contact with all of them, not just the person who asked you the question. You are talking to everyone and need to engage and maintain the interest of the whole group.

Facial expression

Again, you may be nervous, but try not to keep a nervous or worried expression on your face throughout the entire interview. Keep your face relaxed with a slight smile.

Slightly frowning now and again while listening to questions is good as it shows interest and thoughtfulness (but remember to stop frowning after a few seconds). Similarly, slightly nodding your head at the appropriate place while the interviewer speaks can indicate understanding and reinforces the two-way nature of the communication in a non-verbal fashion.

Posture

Your posture should reinforce your verbal and facial signals. In other words it should also be sending the message of relaxed confidence. Sit upright in your chair with your hands resting flat on your thighs or lightly clasped in front of you.

Do NOT tightly grip your hands, wring them, rub them together or generally fiddle with your fingers or rings.

Men should unbutton their jacket when sitting down.

Women should neatly cross their legs. Men shouldn't cross their legs. If men cross their legs vertically like a woman it can make them appear feminine, while if they cross them with one leg horizontal this can appear too casual for an interview situation.

Leaning forward slightly now again is a good way to signal interest in what the interviewer is saying but don't rock backwards and forwards as though in a rocking chair.

Hand and arm gestures

As mentioned above your hands should rest lightly on your lap or the table if you are behind a desk. Avoid crossing your arms.

Hand and arm gestures should be kept to a minimum especially if you do not normally use them. This is not the time to practice amateur dramatics to make what you are saying seem more important or interesting.

Some people seem to have a range of mini hand gestures where they jerk their hand to emphasise what they are saying but the hand never leaves their lap or the table. This should also be avoided.

4 TYPES OF INTERVIEW QUESTIONS

Here I set out 4 common styles or types of questions which may appear in a medical school interview.

If you are aware of the category your question belongs in when you are asked it, it should help to guide you as to the best type of answer to give.

Factual questions

This type of question simply confirms facts, e.g. what subjects did you study at A level? What did you do in your last job?

Opinion questions

These types of questions ask you to give your opinion on a particular subject; e.g. what are your strengths and weaknesses? What do you think are the qualities of a good doctor?

While asking for your opinions these questions usually do have a right or wrong answer. For example the question above regarding the qualities of a good doctor which definitely has some keywords which you should mention.

These questions are perhaps the easiest type of question to answer since to a large extent many of them can be predicted before the interview and you should immediately be able to give your pre-prepared response.

Ethical cases questions

These questions will pose an ethical dilemma e.g. you have one liver available for transplant, but two patients with equal medical need. One is an ex-alcoholic mother with two young children, the other a 13 year old with an inborn liver abnormality. How would you decide to whom it should be given?

These kinds of questions are not usually interested in your opinion and there isn't usually a right or wrong answer. They are looking for an understanding and awareness of the issues involved and how to apply them to the particular case.

We will be looking at answers to ethical cases later on.

Example based questions

Also called behavioural questions. These questions want you to provide evidence of your answers or achievements with specific examples of what you have done in the past.

In this way the interviewer hopes to separate those who merely say they are goal orientated (for example) but cannot give any past example of when they have achieved a goal, from those who can provide concrete examples of goals they have achieved and how they achieved them.

Examples of these types of questions are "describe a time in school when you had many projects or assignments due at the same time. What steps did you take to get them all done?"

Or

"Describe a situation where you found yourself dealing with someone who didn't like you. How did you handle it?"

As you prepare for your interviews and as you work through the questions in this book you should constantly be asking yourself "is this an example question?" "Could I be asked to back this up with a specific example?"

It may seem impossible to have examples prepared for the hundreds of different types of questions you could be asked, however you will soon see that most questions are variations around common themes. You will realise that you only need a few examples which you will be able to adapt to most situations.

Top 10 Questions

As reported by candidates from actual interviews.

Here are some of the most frequently asked questions. Study them well, chances are, one or more of them will come up in your interview.

Why do you want to be a doctor?

Obviously you have your reasons, otherwise you wouldn't have applied to do medicine. Articulating those reasons in a sensible way however is another thing entirely.

Here are some things you should not say –

"To help people" – this answer will just lead to you being asked "Why not another job where you can help people such as nursing?"

"Because I'm interested in science" – as above will lead to you being asked, "Why not do a science degree?"

It is much better to focus on your own particular skills and attributes and relate them to a career in medicine. You can then combine things such as "wanting to work in a caring profession" within this answer to build an overall picture that points towards being a doctor.

For example –

"When choosing a career I thought about the things I enjoy and my particular skills. I enjoy working with people and I believe I have good communication skills, the ability to work in a team and the necessary commitment for medicine. My work experience in a local hospital showed me that I would enjoy working in a caring profession and medicine would allow me to do this while at the same time provide sufficient scope for intellectual and professional development."

This answer shows that you have thought about the skills needed by a doctor, have thought about whether you possess those skills and have also taken positive steps in the form of undertaking work experience to confirm your choice.

What attributes are necessary in a good doctor?

Have you thought about what qualities are needed in a doctor? Do you have those qualities? Be prepared for follow up questions asking you for examples of the last time you demonstrated those qualities.

The British Medical Association lists the following core attributes of a good doctor –

- *Competence*

- *Integrity*

- *Confidentiality*

- *Caring*

- *Compassion*

- *Commitment*

- *Responsibility*

- *Advocacy*

- *Spirit of enquiry*

Of these "competence" is the most important since an incompetent doctor could harm his patients.

To the above list could be added good communication skills, ability to work in a team, ability to deal with stress etc.

What do you think you will be the positive aspects and the negative aspects of being a doctor?

This question tests your understanding of the realities of working as a doctor, both the good and bad aspects. Although the interviewers will probably be more interested in your grasp of the negative aspects to weed out candidates with an overly romantic view of medicine and who may believe they will spend their time sitting around discussing interesting medical cases with a Hugh Laurie look-alike with a limp.

Positive aspects:

- *Opportunity to serve the public / satisfaction from helping people*

- *Challenge*

- *Responsibility*

- *Interesting*

- *Dynamic – constant developments in medical knowledge*

- *Varied types of work / flexibility in future career paths*

Negative aspects:

- *Long training*

- *Uncertainty in work i.e. not knowing if diagnosis/treatment is correct or will have desired outcome.*

- *Constant learning and need to keep professional knowledge up to date*

- *Long hours*

- *Difficult working conditions – e.g. lack of resources*

- *Political interference in work – e.g. constant changes to NHS, targets etc.*

- *Increasing levels of litigation*

- *Difficult / abusive patients*

Why X University?

For this question you need to do some research for yourself regarding the medical schools you have applied to. Of course, you did this at the time of making your applications right?

As previously mentioned, the university web site, prospectus, and any other letters or information they have sent you are all good sources of information.

Try to avoid giving simplistic answers which could get you into trouble –

You: "I chose this university because it has a good reputation."

Interviewer: "Which medical schools do think don't have good reputations?"

You: "I chose this university because it has a PBL based course."

Interviewer: "Why not X, Y or Z universities which also have PBL courses?"

Or worse, because you didn't do your homework –

Interviewer: "Actually we run a traditional course here."

Just like your answer to the question "Why do you want to be a doctor" it is better to give an integrated answer which shows you have considered various factors.

Also do not be afraid to include as one of your reasons the fact that a particular university is close to home and may be cheaper for you to attend than another one. Medical school is a big financial commitment and the fact that you have thought about this will surely not count against you.

A suggested answer –

"I prefer a traditional / PBL based course (delete as appropriate) because it fits better with my personal learning style. Having attended the open day here I decided I liked both the course and the atmosphere of this university and would feel comfortable studying here. Also studying here means I'm closer to home which helps me out financially."

Of course, be prepared to justify exactly why you prefer traditional or PBL based courses or what exactly you like about the atmosphere of the university e.g. friendly people, plenty of extra-curricular interests (not trivial since you will spend 4/5 years there and need some way of de-stressing) etc.

Also be aware that the interviewers may have your application form available to them. If you have applied to several universities, some of which have PBL courses and others traditional courses be prepared to explain this e.g.

"While I'd prefer to do a PBL/traditional course that is not the only factor in my choice hence I have taken other factors into account in my choice to apply to Y university."

Tell us about any medical articles you have seen in the media recently.

This a frequent question and "recent" should mean no more than a month old, otherwise you'll look like you hardly ever read medical articles.

If you are not already doing so make it a habit to seek out medical articles, especially as you get closer to the interview date. This doesn't necessarily mean you have to order The Lancet every month, but at least read the science pages of a quality newspaper. Any important medical stories will certainly be featured there.

Before your interview, pick one which you think you can talk about comfortably and give your opinion on. Try to anticipate if there are any follow up questions they could ask you.

What do you consider to be important advances in medicine over the last 50 / 100 years?

This question is again testing the genuineness of your interest in medicine and your understanding of important public health issues.

In any question regarding important advances in medicine or public health the first thing you should always demonstrate awareness of is the fact that the greatest number of lives have been saved not by great scientific breakthroughs but by simple things such as the provision of clean drinking water and improvements in nutrition.

Drinking water only began to be chlorinated in the 19th century leading in particular to cases of typhoid dysentery and cholera plummeting.

The biochemist Casimir Funk introduced the term vitamine in 1912. Researchers later identified vitamins needed by the body to prevent deficiency diseases such as beriberi, rickets, scurvy, and pellagra. As nutrition has improved these diseases have virtually disappeared from developed countries.

Other important advances in medicine have been –

- In 1796 British physician Edward Jenner introduced vaccination to prevent smallpox

- French physician René-Théophile-Hyacinthe Laënnec invented the stethoscope in 1819

- In 1842 Crawford Long in the United States discovered the anaesthetic effects of ether. The use of anaesthetics enabled surgeons to perform longer operations and reduced surgical mortality.

- Louis Pasteur developed the Germ Theory of Disease in the 1860s, which was the first recognition that microorganisms cause disease in humans.

- Joseph Lister, influenced by the Germ Theory of Disease began using carbolic acid as the first antiseptic in the late 1860s. At that time post-operative sepsis infection accounted for the death of almost half of the patients undergoing major surgery.

- German and French scientists in the1930s showed that sulphonamide was effective in treating streptococcal bacteria infections. This discovery led to the development of antibiotics.

- In 1953 Francis Crick and James Watson identified the double-helix structure of deoxyribonucleic acid (DNA) which allowed us to understand how DNA carries genetic information and its role in genetic diseases.

- In 2003 scientists completed the sequence of the human genome.

Any idea what field within medicine you want to do?

The best answer to this question is not to commit yourself to any particular speciality for two reasons –

1. It could make it appear that you don't have a genuine interest in medicine, just a small area. Since you will spend your whole time at med school studying general medicine rather than any speciality, and likewise in the early part of your working career this doesn't make you an ideal candidate for the course.

2. It could make you appear as though you have an unrealistic attitude to your future career. Until you have actually had some experience of what is involved in different areas of medicine it is very difficult to make an informed choice between them. If you appear to have committed yourself too firmly without having had any actual experience first you will appear naïve.

It is much better to give a non-committal answer such as –

"No, I don't want to close any doors at this early stage. I think it's better to wait and get experience of different areas of medicine to get a realistic idea of what's involved and see which areas I enjoy the most, then I can make an informed decision."

What causes you stress? How do you deal with stress?

Working as a doctor can undoubtedly be stressful. Whether it is more stressful than any number of other professional careers is debatable, however your interviewers are certainly not interested in that debate.

They want to see that you are a person who recognises that they suffer from stress at times and have strategies to cope with your stress. Do not say you don't suffer from stress or that you thrive on stress or you will immediately fail this question.

For what causes you stress talk about the usual subjects such as exams, having to meet work deadlines etc. Now is not the moment to mention any strange personal foibles, stick to non-controversial things.

For dealing with stress you should talk about how you make an effort to regularly play sports, have other interests to take your mind off problems, have a good network of friends to discuss problems with, etc etc.

How has your work experience affected you?

Many med schools place great emphasis on applicants gaining relevant work experience in a health care setting. Even if your chosen med schools do not specifically mention it as a requirement in their prospectuses it can only help your application to have some work experience in this field.

Most applicants gain such experience by working as volunteers in local hospitals or nursing homes.

Many hospitals will also allow you to "shadow" a consultant for a week to gain an insight into their work. This can usually be arranged by contacting the voluntary services department.

A common mistake when answering questions about work experience is to talk in purely observational terms, and focusing exclusively on the doctors e.g.

"… I saw the doctors do this and I saw them do that. They were very caring and helpful etc etc…"

Unfortunately this type of answer does not demonstrate that you have learned much on a personal level from your experience about your own suitability for a career in medicine.

Here is a suggested answer which demonstrates the candidate is aware of how her experience has positively affected her –

"Well, first of all I learnt that I didn't mind being around sick people all day and that I could actually work in that sort of environment. I think I got a realistic idea of a doctor's day to day work but also an appreciation of the extent to which doctors work in health teams. The work of the nurses and other hospital staff was just as important to the patients as that of the doctors and I got a good idea of how important it is for all members of the team to communicate and work together effectively."

"I think I also gained an understanding of issues which can affect patients during their stay in hospital. Many of them feel frustrated by their lack of control over their

environment, for example they cannot decide when they get up, what time they have their meals etc. many may also feel lonely or isolated being separated from their families as well as going through the stress and uncertainty of suffering from an illness."

If you were in a team of doctors and a colleague was not doing the job well what would you do?

This questions is testing your ability to deal with problems arising within a team as well as your willingness to put the patients interests first even if this means informing on a colleague.

Suggested answer –

"I would try and discuss the problem with the colleague first of all to discover if there was any way to resolve the problem. Perhaps the person concerned needs further training or doesn't fully understand the job requirements. If the problem continued then I would have to discuss the matter with a more senior member of the team."

Top 5 Interview Mistakes

Failing to create a dialogue

When you go to an interview you expect to be asked questions. But don't forget, this is not an interrogation where you must just passively answer the questions put to you. You should think of the interview as an exchange between equals.

This means creating a dialogue between yourself and the interviewers. Ask questions of them if necessary to clarify questions and seek further information about what they are really asking you about. This will help create a more relaxed atmosphere more akin to a real conversation, which in turn will help you to relax and improve your performance.

To be honest

If you are one of those people who tends to use phrases such as "To be honest…" or "To tell you the truth…." Before answering questions then I suggest that you eliminate them from your vocabulary along with any other verbal tics or repetitive phrases you habitually use.

Not only is it annoying for an interviewer to hear the same phrase preceding every answer but even if only used once in your interview the phrase "To be honest…." can create a bad impression.

Why do you need to say that? Does it mean your other answers haven't been honest? In short it can make you look shifty, so avoid it.

There are plenty of other phrases which are OK if used once or twice but can become annoying if they precede every answer e.g. "Well…" "Errrm" etc.

Tell us about yourself

This is a typical question which at first sight seems quite easy to answer. After all, it doesn't require any difficult technical or scientific knowledge. It only requires you to talk about yourself, what could be easier than that?

Unfortunately, in practice this question is surprisingly badly answered by many candidates. The main reason for this mistake is that candidates have failed to think beforehand about their key attributes which they want the interviewers to know about.

Let's see a really poor answer given by an anonymous candidate –

Interviewer – "Tell us about yourself."

Anonymous candidate - "I like cats."

Now let's look at a typical answer given by a poor candidate, we'll call her Lucy –

Interviewer – "Tell us about yourself."

Lucy – "Well, I'm 20 years old, I studied chemistry, physics and biology for my A levels, which I really enjoyed and then after school I decided I'd had enough of studying for a while so I took a gap year and decided to travel around Australia which was fantastic……."

Oh dear, I think we can all see what's wrong with Lucy's answer. She began by telling the interviewers what she studied for her A levels which they could have just read from her application form anyway, she then went on to tell them about her gap year in purely personal terms without relating the experience in any way to her future career or personal development.

Now let's see a better answer from Sue –

"I'm quite an organised person, while I was doing my A levels I also did some voluntary work in a local hospital so I had to learn to timetable my studies effectively around my voluntary work and other hobbies. I feel I managed this quite well because my A level results were very good.

I also think I've been able to develop quite good communication skills, I've just come back from my gap year in Australia. I travelled all round the country and had to talk to lots of different people from different backgrounds and cultures.

Finally I like to think that I'm a caring person which is part of the reason I want to become a doctor."

As you can see, Sue's answer is undoubtedly more effective. You should think about your own unique selling points and experience which might be relevant to medicine and have a pre-prepared answer similar to Sue's which will allow you to really sell yourself to the interviewers if you are asked this or a similar question.

What's your greatest weakness?

This question has become such a hackneyed interview question that you may have difficulty suppressing a smile at the interviewers lack of imagination if it crops up in your interview.

The standard response to this question is to give a characteristic which can also be a strength e.g.

"I pay a lot of attention to small details which means I sometimes miss the bigger picture."

Or

"I can be impatient with people who are not as committed as me."

Unfortunately these sorts of answers have become as hackneyed as the question itself and it is a mistake to use any response along these lines.

The interviewers will hear this sort of answer over and over again and you will appear unoriginal and rehearsed.

As a first response to this sort of question I suggest an answer like this –

"I don't think I'm perfect but I don't think I have any major flaws that would hinder my ability to work as a doctor. However I know there's always room for improvement so I'm open to constructive criticism."

If you are pressed further, mention a genuine weakness but show that you are aware of it and have attempted to do something about it. Stay away from personal character traits (e.g. I lose my temper easily) and only mention professional/work characteristics as your weakness. Also do NOT mention any of the characteristics of a good doctor which I gave earlier, make sure you know these and don't mention ANY of them as a weakness.

Here's a suggested answer –

"I know my computer skills are a bit weak which is why I attended a computer course last month to improve my word processing knowledge."

Or

"I do get stressed when I have a lot of work to do but I do have coping strategies for this, in particular I find exercise helps me relax and I always get back to my work with renewed energy after a workout."

Complaining

Complaining of any kind in an interview is a bad mistake. Yet it is a trap which is all too easy to fall into.

When asked to explain, for example, poor performance in exams or why you left a job it is all too easy to begin blaming teachers or tutors or to criticise a previous boss.

Even if your criticisms are perfectly justified, in an interview situation these answers will just make you appear like a whinger who doesn't take responsibility. And no one likes a whinger.

Stay positive about all your past experiences. If there have been genuine problems acknowledge them briefly without blaming others, then move swiftly on to how you have learnt from the experience.

Relaxation Techniques

Here's a couple of techniques which you can use before your interview to calm your nerves. Try them, they really work! In fact the second one can even be used during the interview if you feel yourself starting to get too nervous.

The Calming Image Technique

Your body responds to its environment and a calm and soothing environment causes the body to relax, heart rate to drop, breathing to become shallower and slower and your mind to feel peaceful.

But it is not necessary to actually change your environment to experience these effects. Experimentation has shown that the body can respond in the same way just by imagining yourself in a calm environment or situation.

How does this work?

Close your eyes and imagine a setting were you feel particularly comfortable and peaceful. You may imagine yourself lying in a field on a summers day listening to the sounds of the birds, or you may imagine yourself on a sandy beach, or maybe next to waterfall on a river listening to the relaxing patter of the water on stones.

Now really imagine yourself there, how does your body feel? For example if you are on a beach imagine how the warm sand feels beneath your back, imagine the heat of the sun's rays on your face, perhaps there is a cooling breeze playing over your body. Now imagine in as much detail as possible your surroundings, listen to the sound of the waves breaking on the beach, look at the palm trees surrounding you, imagine every detail.

As you continue this process you will find yourself becoming more and more relaxed.

The good thing about this technique is that it works better the more you use it. This is because your body becomes trained to relax as you begin your imagery and gradually responds faster and better to you beginning the technique.

The Squeeze and Breathe Technique

This is a quick and simple physical technique to help you control any feelings of physical nervousness such as shaking or breathlessness.

First, take a deep breath in through your nose and just as your lungs fill to capacity begin to squeeze your stomach muscles hard, (but not too hard it makes you want to expel your lunch). Now while squeezing your stomach slowly breathe out through your nose.

Doing this a couple of times helps to relax the body and normalise your breathing.

It can be done discretely, so you could even do it during the interview if you began to feel too nervous.

In any case if you do feel so nervous in the interview that you begin to stutter or don't get your words out properly, don't be afraid to stop in mid answer, do the "squeeze and breathe" to regain your composure and then continue.

The interviewers will see you are nervous but will also see that you are able to control it, which shouldn't count against you.

The Repeating the Question Technique

There are two ways to use this technique –

1. If you didn't hear the question properly or think you didn't understand it properly then rather than just asking the interviewer to repeat it try paraphrasing the question in your own words. You can preface this with a question such as

"So what you are asking is………?" Or

"Do you mean………"

This is always preferable to answering the question you *think* was asked rather than the question actually asked. It may also prompt the interviewer to word the question in a slightly different way and thus give you more information on which to base your answer.

2. This technique can also be used to buy yourself a few seconds of time to think of an answer if you are asked a difficult question. If you repeat the question smoothly immediately after being asked it, it won't appear at all like you are trying to buy time.

THE PUTTING IT IN CONTEXT PLOY

Imagine you are asked a difficult question. You are not sure how to answer.

Your first response should be to use the "Repeating the Question Technique" to paraphrase the question and buy a few extra seconds.

But then, you still cannot think of how to answer. Fortunately there is another method you can use to gain a few more seconds to think of an answer. The beauty of this technique is that even if you cannot think of a good answer afterwards, the technique itself makes it seem that you appreciate why the question was asked.

The technique involves putting the question you are asked into context before answering it e.g.

"Yes I understand the importance of that in the context of….."

Let's see how it works with an example –

Interviewer – "Can you give me an example of the last time you used good communication skills?"

You (trying the Repeating the Question Technique first) – "So do you mean how I've used communication skills to achieve a satisfactory result in a particular situation?"

Interviewer – "Yes, exactly."

You (now falling back on the Putting It In Context Ploy) – "Yes, I can appreciate the importance of communication skills in the context of working as a doctor because it will be essential to communicate well with patients and colleagues. (At this point you begin to think of an answer) I suppose the best example I can give you is……….."

66 Typical Questions

With some suggested answers

66 of the most commonly asked questions as reported by candidates from actual interviews organized by the following categories:

The medical school
The course
Motivation for medicine
Appreciation of the realities of medicine
Medical work experience
Other work experience (non health related)
Interest in medicine
Personal qualities & achievements
Personal interests
Experience & knowledge of teamwork
Communication skills
Self awareness & personal development
Knowledge of NHS
Population health
Gender & cultural awareness
Issues involved in research

The medical school

What interests you about the curriculum at [Medical School]? When you read the [Medical School] prospectus, what appealed to you or interested you in the course here?

This is very similar to the "Why do you want to come to this University?" question we have seen in the top 10 questions section, however this question focuses exclusively on the academic curriculum.

You will need to have done your research on the universities you have applied to in order to be able to answer this question intelligently. As suggested before check the university web-site and paper prospectus for information.

Some particular areas you could mention are –

- PBL, integrated or traditional course

- Opportunities for clinical placements on wards/in the community

- Emphasis on self directed learning

- Opportunities to do Special Study Modules

- Taught by practising doctors and by clinical and scientific academics

- Electives abroad

- Opportunity to study an intercalated BSc

What do you think are the advantages and disadvantages of coming to medical school?

Advantages –

- First step in your professional career

- Opportunity to study something you are genuinely interested in

- Opportunity to meet & learn from practising medics

- Opportunity to benefit from and contribute to university life by membership of clubs and societies

- Meeting new people and making new friends

- Social life

Disadvantages

- Hard work

- Expense

- May have to move house

- Being away from friends and family

How will you contribute to [X] university?

"First of all by being a good student and upholding the high academic standards for which the university is known. Secondly, I look forward to contributing to university life and events such as raising money for charity during Rag Week. Finally I think it is important to participate in university societies and sports clubs, I'm a keen squash player and that is one club I'd be very interested in joining."

The course

What do you know about PBL? Why do you want to come to a PBL medical school?

The aim of PBL (Problem Based Learning) is to provide a context for what is being learned. It involves a practical clinical case being presented to the students in the form of a patient presenting with a particular problem.

Working in small groups the students discuss amongst themselves what they need to learn in order to understand and solve the problem and decide a common set of learning objectives to be reported back on at the next session.

A tutor is usually present in the sessions but he does not teach or tell the students the "answer". The tutor's role is to act as a facilitator guiding the discussion to relevant areas.

PBL suits students who are self-motivated and are capable of self-directed learning rather than being taught through traditional methods such as lectures. PBL students enjoy problem solving and teamwork.

The material studied may seem more relevant through always being directly related to a "real" patient or problem and so may be easier to remember than just learning isolated facts.

What do you think are the advantages and disadvantages of a PBL course?

Advantages –

- Based on realistic scenarios so material studied seems relevant and may be easier to remember

- Its interactive nature makes learning process more interesting

- Mimics actual working conditions of working in a clinical team and needing to discuss the best course of action for a patient and so is good preparation for working life

- Develops ability to make judgements when faced with uncertainty

- Helps build team working and interpersonal skills

- Helps build professional skills such as making presentations to colleagues

- The group acts as a learning resource as all members share their knowledge

- Helps develop lifelong learning skills

Disadvantages

- May be an inefficient way to learn as the learning objectives chosen by the group may not be relevant to the problem, or may be set too wide or too narrow and will need to be revised in subsequent sessions

- Some members of the group may not pull their weight leading to most of the work always being done by the same people

- There may be conflicts and disagreements within the group about the learning objectives which need to be set or about other matters

- Members of the group with a strong personality may dominate discussions and unduly influence the group with their ideas (which may be incorrect)

This course will require a good deal of independent study, how have you managed this approach to learning in the past?

At some stage in the past you must have had some experience of independent study, whether it was just doing your private study for A levels, or studying for BMAT, MCAT or GAMSAT. Perhaps you even have some experience of PBL from a previous degree.

Keywords to mention are time management, planning and self-motivation.

E.g.

"In the past I've found that to be effective my private study periods had to be well planned. I had to have decided the important topics to be covered in a session

before the session began. Time management was also important to ensure I completed what I had planned to do in the time available."

What previous experiences have you had of learning in a small group setting?

If you haven't had any previous experiences of this type of learning you could say –

"My previous academic experience has been in large groups. One of the reasons I'm interested in this course is the opportunity to experience a new teaching method."

However before you deny ever having worked in a small group think about all of your past academic experiences whether formal or otherwise. Have you ever done any study with a group of friends when revising for exams at school or university? Or were you ever required to work in small groups or discuss work in any of your classes. If so then you do have some experience which you can use for your answer.

E.g.

"When revising for my A levels / university exams I used to have revision sessions with a few friends. I found that talking about the work with other people made the learning process more active and memorising facts became easier."

Motivation for medicine

What do you want to achieve in medicine?

"My priority at the moment is to gain a place at medical school and to be a successful medical student. Then to become the best doctor I can be and progress professionally to finally become a consultant or GP. Until I decide what speciality I'd like to do in the future it's difficult to be more specific at this stage."

What have you read or experienced in order to prepare you for medicine?

Many med schools expect you to have made an effort to get some work experience in a health related setting. If you have then this question is your opportunity to mention this.

If not then think of any other work experience you have which may be relevant. Any work involving contact with the public or working in a team will have some relevance to medicine and you can mention the skills you learned in the job and how they are transferable to medicine.

E.g.

"I did voluntary work one day a week in a local hospital last year. I didn't have that much contact with the doctors but the experience did give me a realistic insight into the daily routine on a ward and what it might be like to work there.

I also had plenty of patient contact which I enjoyed

and I think it helped me understand some of the issues which patients in hospital have to deal with in hospital apart from their illness e.g. loneliness, lack of control over environment, worrying about who is looking after their dog while they are in hospital, worrying about how they will cope when they leave hospital if they are still incapacitated etc.

I've also worked as a [waiter/supermarket checkout person/lawyer/journalist] which involved dealing with the public and so it helped develop my communication skills which are important in medicine as well. It also gave me useful experience of working in a team with other people which again is important in medicine since doctors work as part of a health care team.

Regarding things I've read to prepare myself, I've read the sections on both the GMC and BMA web sites about medical careers and I downloaded the pdf document available on the BMA web site called "Becoming a Doctor" and I also bought the book "The Essential Guide To Becoming a Doctor" which gives information on the training and working conditions."

"Becoming a Doctor" – available free from the BMA here –

http://www.bma.org.uk/careers/becoming_doctor/index.jsp

"The Essential Guide To Becoming a Doctor" – available from the Gamsat Review Bookstore here –

http://astore.amazon.co.uk/griffithsgams-21/detail/0470654554

Why do you believe you have the ability to undertake the study and work involved?

"I think that the academic results I've achieved so far show that I am definitely capable of the study and work necessary. Although medicine will be a new subject for me I believe that the study skills I already possess should enable me to make satisfactory progress."

Why do you want to be a doctor, rather than another profession that is caring or intellectually challenging?
Why don't you want to be a nurse?
What aspect of healthcare attracts you to medicine?

"Medicine combines both the caring aspects of other health professions with greater intellectual challenge. Doctors need a deeper understanding of the physiology of the human body than other health care professionals such as nurses. In addition doctors perform functions which cannot be done by others such as the diagnosis of illness and prescribing treatments and medications."

If you were to become a doctor, how would you wish your patients to describe you and why?

See the list of desirable attributes for a doctor given above.

What relevance to medicine are the 'A' levels (apart from biology and chemistry) that you have been studying?

If you studied statistics you could mention that it is

useful for interpreting data from trials and studies which is applicable when evaluating new drugs and treatments or when studies are done to assess the health of a population or the incidence of a particular disease.

If you studied physics it is very possible that you had a medical physics module and even if you didn't you will be able to talk about how general physics knowledge would enable you to better understand certain medical devices.

For example knowledge of waves is relevant to ultrasound scanning. Knowledge of radiation is relevant to X rays and radiotherapy treatment for cancer. Knowledge of electric currents may help in understanding transmission of nerve impulses. Knowledge of stress and force aids understanding of bone fractures etc.

If the subjects you studied were really nothing to do with medicine then you could say something like –

"Well I'm studying Russian and French which aren't directly relevant, however the grades I'm getting do show that I have the ability to study difficult subjects to a high level and give me confidence that I'll be able to cope with the workload of a medical degree."

What is integrity?

"Firm adherence to a code of moral or ethical values"

When was the last time you acted with integrity?

If you have some interesting story about how someone tried to bribe you, or how you informed on your best friend for cheating in an exam then mention it, if not then try this –

"I believe integrity isn't necessarily just displayed by some big gesture or heroic act but should be a personal quality that we display in our day to day life and in the way we treat other people. For example today I paid my bus fare to get here, even though it's very easy to get on London buses without paying nowadays. In this interview I am trying to be truthful in the answers I give, even though it may be tempting to exaggerate or embellish certain things. Integrity is a personal approach to life."

What is empathy?

"The ability to share someone else's feelings or experiences by imagining what it would be like to be in their situation"

Appreciation of the realities of medicine

What do you think being a doctor entails, apart from treating patients?

The GMC lists the duties of a doctor as –

- make the care of your patient your first concern;

- treat every patient politely and considerately;

- respect patients' dignity and privacy;

- listen to patients and respect their views;

- give patients information in a way they can understand;

- respect the rights of patients to be fully involved in decisions about their care;

- keep your professional knowledge and skills up to date;

- recognise the limits of your professional competence;

- be honest and trustworthy;

- respect and protect confidential information;

- make sure that your personal beliefs do not prejudice your patients' care;

- act quickly to protect patients from risk if you have good reason to believe that you or a colleague may not be fit to practise;

- avoid abusing your position as a doctor; and

- work with colleagues in the ways that best serve patients' interests.

What do GP's do apart from treating patients?

- Liasing with other health professionals e.g. District Nurses and Health Visitors

- Training other doctors – i.e. GP registrars

- Keeping their own training up to date

- Financial, planning and controlling the monetary aspect of running a practice

When you think about becoming a doctor, what do you look forward to most and least?

See question about advantages and disadvantages of being a doctor.

What steps have you taken to try to find out whether you really do want to become a doctor?

Things you can mention –

- Health related work experience

- Shadowing a GP or hospital doctor

- Talking to doctors

- Reading

What things do you think might make people inclined to drop out of medical training?

"If someone did not have a realistic idea of the demands of a career in medicine before they started or had not taken

steps to be sure they really wanted to work in medicine, such as gaining relevant work experience, then this could lead to them dropping out."

If asked what those demands are see list of negative points about being a doctor given above.

How would you dissuade someone from going into Medicine?

See list of negative points about being a doctor given above.

How old are you when you become a consultant? Describe the path after medical school

These sorts of questions are testing your knowledge of the career path of a doctor.

The system is currently undergoing changes with a view to modernising doctors training under a program called Modernising Medical Careers (MMC) which from 2005 will see the Pre Registration House Officer and Senior House Officer Posts become Foundation Years 1 and 2.

Under the new scheme after Foundation Year 2, doctors will be either enter specialist training immediately (Specialist Registrar) or undertake a further 2 years training in either Core Medical Training or Core Surgical Training. Which of these routes they take will depend on the specialty they wish to enter since there are different requirements for each specialty.

However, the final scheme will probably be as follows –

- **Medical School** – 4 to 6 years

- **Foundation Years 1&2**

Then either:

- **Specialist Registrar** – 5-6 years training in a chosen speciality. On completion of further exams set by Royal medical colleges become a Consultant, or **GP Registrar** – 5 years training to become a GP. On completion of further exams become a GP Principal.

Or

- **Core Training** – 2 years further training in either medicine or surgery and then enter specialist training as above.

So in total it could be a further 7+ years after medical school to become a hospital consultant or a GP.

You should be aware however that this is an area subject to continuing change.

Who do you register with after F1 (PRHO) year?

You register with the GMC. During your first year working in a hospital you only have provisional registration with the GMC. After successful completion of the F1 year you gain full registration as a doctor.

What do GMC, BMA, RCS mean?

GMC – General Medical Council. It regulates doctors and maintains the register of doctors allowed to practice in the UK.

BMA – British Medical Association. It is the doctor's trade union representing the interests of individual doctors and the profession as a whole.

RCS – Royal College of Surgeons. It supervises the training of surgeons.

Medical work experience

What steps have you taken to try to find out whether you really do want to become a doctor? What experiences have given you insight into the world of medicine? What have you learnt from these?

See answers given above

Reflect on what you have seen of hospitals or a health care environment. What would you most like to organise differently, and why? Have you visited any friends or family in hospital, or had work experience in a hospital? From these experiences, what did you see that you would like to change?

Obviously no criticism should be made of any of the

hospital staff in response to this question whether it be of doctors, nurses or anyone else.

Try and think of something you have seen that can be criticised without causing offence e.g. the building was very old, the nurses worked very hard but seemed to be understaffed, lack of facilities for patients etc.

Can you think of a specific case from your work experience that confirmed your desire to be a doctor?

If there was then tell them about it.

If not (and don't feel there has to be) say–

"There wasn't an actual Eureka moment which hit me but the work experience as a whole has confirmed my desire and over the course of my time there I became gradually more convinced that I'm making the right decision."

Other work experience (non health related)

In your work experience, what skills have you learnt that you can apply to medicine?

This will obviously vary according to the exact nature of your employment but some skills which could have been acquired that could be transferable to medicine are listed below –

- Communication skills

- Teamwork skills

- Organisational ability

- Time management

- Responsibility

- IT skills

- Problem solving skills

Can you give me an example of how you coped with a conflict with a colleague or friend; what strategy did you use and why?

"When I disagree with someone my first strategy is to explain my point of view in a different way as the other person may have misunderstood what I mean. I also ask the other person to explain their point of view in a different way by asking them to clarify exactly what they mean. Sometimes we can then find some middle ground between our two positions.

If no agreement results getting the opinion or advice of a third party can sometimes be useful."

Thinking of your work experience, can you tell me about a difficult situation you have dealt with and what you learned from it?

Avoid talking about any problems about working with other people or colleagues. Stick to professional situations such as meeting deadlines, dealing with difficult customers or computer crashes etc.

The way you dealt with the problem should show that you recognised the problem quickly and came up with a solution.

Tell me about a project, or work experience, that you have organised, and what you learned from it?

You should relate what you learned to the qualities necessary in a doctor. A safe generalised answer which you can also add in this situation is to say –

"I learnt that it's always better to ask a question even if I think it makes me look stupid than to risk making a mistake later on through ignorance. I also learnt not to over commit myself and that it's better to promise less but deliver more."

Interest in medicine

Tell us about Hippocrates.

"Hippocrates, known as the Father of modern medicine, was a Greek physician born in 460 BC on the island of Cos, Greece. Rejecting the superstitions of his time he held the belief that illness had a physical and a rational explanation. He accurately described disease symptoms and was the first physician to accurately describe the symptoms of pneumonia. He founded a medical school and developed an Oath of Medical Ethics for physicians to follow. He died in 377 BC."

What do you think was the greatest public health advance of the twentieth century?

As mentioned previously the greatest public health advance has been the provision of clean drinking water, followed by improved nutrition.

Drinking water only began to be chlorinated in the 19th century leading in particular to cases of typhoid dysentery and cholera plummeting.

The biochemist Casimir Funk introduced the term vitamine in 1912. Researchers later identified vitamins needed by the body to prevent deficiency diseases such as beriberi, rickets, scurvy, and pellagra. As nutrition has improved these diseases have virtually disappeared from developed countries.

How do you think the rise in information technology has influenced / will influence the practice of medicine?

"Computers are impacting all areas of medicine. Modern imaging machines can only be operated and create images with the help of a computer to analyse the data. As medicine becomes more specialised diagnosis and treatment is increasingly carried out by different doctors. Computerisation of patient records enables them to share information and communicate effectively. Finally as medical knowledge increases at an ever-faster rate there is an increasing requirement for doctors to continue their professional education. Computer based techniques and resources are increasingly being used to achieve this."

Personal qualities & achievements

Why should we choose you?

"I believe I have the necessary personal and academic qualities to succeed at medical school and to go on to be a good doctor.

I'm a competent person in the sense that I if I need to do something I can usually do it well. I think my [academic results/career achievements/sporting achievements/ other achievements] demonstrate this. I think this is one of the most important qualities for a doctor since an incompetent doctor could put lives at risk.

I'm also a person who cares about the well being of others which again I think you can see from my [voluntary work/charity collections/involvement in student unions or as student representative]

I've also made an effort to ensure I have a realistic idea of what working as a doctor is really like through my work experience at my local hospital. This helped me to gain an appreciation of a doctor's work and some of the issues which affect doctors working conditions.

The experience convinced me I would enjoy being a doctor and gave me even more motivation to become one, which is why I think you should give me a chance to study at your medical school."

Can you tell us about any particular life experiences that you think may help or hinder you in a career in medicine?

Another opportunity to talk about your work experience in a health care setting, or skills you have gained from employment, or study skills, or teamwork skills whether gained from work or playing sports.

"I've also worked as a [waiter/supermarket checkout person/lawyer/journalist] which involved dealing with the public and so it helped develop my communication skills which are very important in medicine. I also improved my organisational and time management skills as well as learning to work effectively as part of a team.

My academic experience so far and the exams I've had to take helped me to learn self directed study skills which will be important not only during my time at medical school but also later in my career when continuous professional development and keeping my skills up to date will be important.

Finally, the voluntary work I did in a local hospital last year gave me a realistic insight into what working in a hospital and caring for sick people is like and has definitely helped prepare me for when I first start working after finishing medical school."

What ways of working and studying have you developed that you think will assist you through medical school? What will you need to improve?

"In both my work and my studies I've learnt that it is very important to plan what I want to achieve before I start any project or study session and I set myself objectives. I've developed quite good time management and so I usually manage to meet the objectives I've set.

If any task takes longer than expected I would prioritise the remaining tasks so that I finish the most important ones first.

I think these are skills which will be important to me at medical school where I will probably have a high workload and will be responsible for my own progress.

I don't think there's anything I need to improve specifically regarding my study skills but if I see I the need to adapt my method of working to suit the specific circumstances of medical school then I will."

What are your outside interests and hobbies? How do these complement you as a person? Which do you think you will continue at university?

Team sports are preferable to mention here as it shows you can get on with other people, however if you play an individual sport like tennis there are also advantages you can mention.

"I play cricket as often as I can. Work and studying are obviously important but so are other aspects of life such as keeping fit and unwinding. Playing in a team means I make a lot of good friends and it's something I'd definitely like to continue playing if I come to university."

"I play tennis as often as I can. Work and studying are obviously important but so are other aspects of life such as keeping fit and unwinding. I like tennis because I can play with my regular opponents but can also play against new people I meet so it's good for my social life too. I'd definitely like to continue playing if I come to university."

Tell us two personal qualities you have which would make you a good doctor, and two personal shortcomings which you think you would like to overcome as you become doctor?

If you could change two things about yourself, what would they be and why?

What qualities do you lack that would be useful for a doctor, and what do you intend to do about this?

What qualities do you think other people value in you?

How do you think other people would describe you?

The "good" personal qualities you mention here should correlate with the desirable qualities of a good doctor given above from the BMA.

"I'm a competent person in the sense that I if I need to do something I can usually do it well. I think my [academic results/career achievements/sporting achievements/ other achievements] demonstrate this. I think this is one of the most important qualities for a doctor since an incompetent doctor could put lives at risk.

I'm also a person who cares about the well being of others which again I think you can see from my [voluntary work/charity collections/involvement in student unions or as student representative]

I'm not perfect but I don't think I have any major personality defects or shortcomings which would hinder my work as a doctor although there's always room for improvement and I'm open to constructive criticism."

I suggest you finish your answer there, but if pressed by the interviewers to give defects or weaknesses say something like -

"For example I do sometimes feel stressed if I have a lot of work to do in a short amount of time but I have coping strategies for dealing with my stress such as good time management at work and unwinding after work by playing sport.

A second one is that I always have a lot of ideas and I don't have any problems about talking in front of other people, so sometimes when working in groups I can monopolise the discussion. I'm aware that this is something I do so I do try and make a conscious effort to hold myself back and let others participate."

Or alternatively –

"I'm a very good listener and sometimes when working in groups I let other people talk more than me. This can sometimes be a problem as I have some good ideas which the group doesn't get to hear. I'm trying to overcome this by always speaking up if I feel I have something important to say."

How will you cope with being criticised or even sued?

"That depends on the reason for the criticism and how the criticism is given. I am always open to constructive criticism and I understand that criticism will be part of my on the job training, however I believe that everyone has the right to work without being insulted or abused. I know that litigation is an increasing problem for doctors

nowadays but I don't think there's anything I can do individually about that except do my own job to the best of my ability."

Personal interests

Have you seen a film or read a book recently that has made you think, and why?

The only important thing when answering this question is that you really have read the book or film. Then if you are asked further questions about it you won't look foolish.

It is probably best to mention a less well known book or film. If the interviewers haven't read or seen it then they can't ask any awkward questions about it.

Tell me about a non-academic project or piece of organisation that you were involved in. How did it go?

It doesn't matter what example you choose here, the only thing that matters is that it shows that you have used important skills.

If you have worked you may have examples of work projects to recount. If not think about any sporting or hobby events you have organised. Even a trip you have organised could be employed to show yourself in a good light.

E.g.

"A couple of months ago a group of us decided to go to London to visit the Science Museum. I volunteered to find out where the museum was and the necessary travel information. I had to plan carefully because we all live in different places and had to leave at different times and travel by different routes to meet up. I researched the train and tube routes and timetables and I made a personalised itinerary for everyone. To my surprise we all met up in the right place and at the right time in London."

What interests do you bring from school/college life that you think will contribute to your studies?

Membership of clubs or societies as well as sports you play are all good things to mention. The interviewers just want to see that you are not a one dimensional character but a well balanced person with a social life.

These things contribute to your studies by helping you relax and de-stress so you can attack your studies with renewed vigour afterwards.

Experience & knowledge of teamwork

Thinking about your membership of a team (in a work, sport, school or other setting), can you tell us about the most important contributions you made to the team?

Modern day health care is very much a team effort. Please tell us a role that you have played in a team, and what you think you contributed. Can you think of a team situation where your communication skills have been vital? Tell us about the situation and your contribution.

"The aim of working in a team is to co operate together to achieve a shared objective. When I work as part of a team my approach is to perform my role in a way which helps the other team members perform their jobs in an efficient fashion. Communication within the team is essential for this process so I always value the opinions of other team members and listen to their ideas."

When you think about yourself working as a doctor, who do you think will be the most important people in the team you will be working with?

"By definition a team is a group of people working together to achieve a common goal. Everyone has their own role to play and the team members are relying on each other. If one person doesn't do their job properly then the team as a whole suffers, so I don't think it's possible to say that any one person is more important than any other in a team situation."

Are you a leader or a follower?

"Effective leadership requires a set of skills and abilities that take time to develop. Anyone who thinks they have nothing more to learn can never be an effective leader. If I felt I had acquired the necessary skills then I wouldn't be afraid to take on positions with more responsibility."

What are the advantages and disadvantages of being in a team? Do teams need leaders?

Advantages –

- Improved morale from working with others

- Mutual encouragement

- Sharing of ideas

- Different abilities of team members complement each other

- Mutual support e.g. one team member can cover for another in case of illness/absence etc.

- Sharing of workload enables more work to be done than working individually

- Builds communication skills

Disadvantages –

- Requires more effort from the members

- Requires more resources e.g. meeting rooms etc

- May be a slower way of working since more discussion/planning is required

- Poor performance from one team member may negatively impact everyone else

- May be harder to apportion responsibility when things go wrong

"A team works best when any plan of action has been arrived at through mutual consensus and the contributions of all the members are given consideration. One person simply telling others what to do cannot be truly called a team. However a team may benefit from someone being given the role of Chairman who acts as a facilitator in group discussions and may have a casting vote in cases of deadlock."

What do you think of nurses developing extended roles and undertaking tasks previously done by doctors?
What do you think are the advantages and disadvantages of nurses replacing doctors as the first contact person in primary care?

"There has probably always been a certain amount of overlap between functions carried out by doctors and nurses. If a nurse is appropriately trained and qualified in a particular procedure or task then there is no reason why that area of overlap should not expand as long as patient care is always the main priority. This may benefit doctors also by reducing their workload and allowing them time for more complicated cases."

Will there be any advantages and disadvantages to the PATIENT if doctors are working in a team?

Advantages –

- More people to care for him

- More constant care i.e. when one team member finishes his shift, another member with knowledge of the patient starts

- More people available with knowledge of the patient

- Sharing of knowledge & experience between the doctors

Disadvantages –

- May be difficult to determine who has overall responsibility for the patient

- Patient may be unsure who is in charge of his treatment

- May be lack of effective communication between the doctors

- Patient may feel he is getting less personal attention from the doctors

- May be disagreements among the doctors

- The more complicated any system becomes, the greater is the likelihood of errors occurring. If a team becomes too large this is a possibility.

Communication skills

What skills do you think are needed in order to communicate with your patients; how do you think they are best acquired?
Can you learn communication skills?

The following are aspects of good communication skills –

- Comfortable atmosphere – introductions etc

- Remove "barriers" e.g. desk between yourself and patient

- Open questions i.e. questions which cannot be answered with a "yes" or "no" e.g. "Tell me about...."

- Listening

- Empathy – demonstrate concern for patients experience

- Confirming – with the use of questions and paraphrasing both that you have understood the patient and that they have understood you e.g. "So what you are saying is....."

- Not interrupting the patient, allow them to finish

- Be aware of non verbal signals

- Don't use medical jargon – use language suitable for a lay person

- Give patient opportunity to ask questions

Communication skills, just like all skills can be taught and learned and the skills acquired can be perfected through practice.

Awareness of barriers to good communication, observing others communicate, having others observe you and give feedback and practising the skills learned are the best ways to achieve good communications skills.

Communication skills are on the curriculum at most (all?) medical schools, so you will need to demonstrate a positive attitude to learning them in the interview.

How have you developed your communication skills?

Here is another question where you can bring in any of your experiences working as part of a team either at work or as part of some academic project or any experience you have had of dealing with the public.

E.g.

"As I mentioned before I've had work experience where I was part of a team and I've also worked on academic projects at school/university with other students. Whenever I work in this type of situation I always try

and develop my communication skills by being sensitive to the needs of the group. I do this by listening to others viewpoints and also by trying to express my own viewpoints as clearly as I can."

What would you prefer in a doctor? Bad communication skills with good clinical skills or good communication skills with bad clinical skills? Why?

"The two skills cannot be separated, communication skills are part of clinical skills. If a doctor does not communicate well with a patient he may not gain all the necessary information in order to make a correct diagnosis"

Self awareness & personal development

When was the last time you had to make a decision without knowing all the facts?

"It is rare to know all the possible facts about every situation before making any kind of decision. Nearly every decision we make in life is based on a set of assumptions. When I decided to take the train here, I did not know if the train driver was drunk or not, or when the brakes on the train had last been checked. Making decisions involves coping with uncertainties and making a judgement about the level of uncertainty you are willing to accept for any particular decision."

Knowledge of NHS

When was the NHS founded?

"The NHS was founded in 1948 by the Labour Prime Minister Aneurin Bevan"

How has the NHS revolutionised medicine?

"Unlike the previous situation which existed in the UK and still exists today in many other countries the NHS makes health care free at the point of use for everyone and is financed by central taxation."

What is wrong with the NHS?
What problems are there in the NHS other than the lack of funding?

Ageing population – as the demographic make up of the population changes and an ever increasing proportion of the population is composed of the elderly the cost to the NHS continues to rise. Older people simply get ill more often as well as suffer from more long term and chronic health problems which can be costly to treat.

Increasing cost of modern treatments and drugs – technological advances have led to significantly improved methods of diagnosis and treatment but this comes at a price, modern scanners for example CAT scanners can cost millions of pounds. New drugs can cost thousands of pounds a year to treat a single patient.

New demands placed on its resources e.g. infertility treatment – new treatment options which were not available before place an extra strain on resources.

Long waiting lists

Regional variations in health care – e.g. some drugs treatments not available in some places, but available in others.

Staff shortages – nurses and doctors.

Administrative and management problems – with any organisation as large and complex as the NHS the task of administration and management will always be complex and subject to problems.

Population health

In what ways do you think doctors can promote good health, other than direct treatment of illness?

Preventative medicine is an important part of a doctor's role. Illness can be prevented by a variety of methods –

- vaccination

- education about risks e.g. of sunbathing, smoking, drinking

- promotion of healthy lifestyles e.g. healthy eating and benefits of exercise"

- through personal example

What does the current government see as the national priorities in health care? Do you agree with these?

- Shorter waiting times

- Giving patients more choice about how, when and where they receive treatment implemented via the "Choose and Book" system by which patients choose the time date and place of appointments and book online when referred to a specialist by their GP.

- Improving the organisation of emergency care

- Cleaner hospitals

If asked what you think of particular reforms be careful to avoid giving political views or criticising government policy since you do not know if the interviewers will agree with you.

It is best to put the answer in terms of "I have read some criticisms of the reforms because…." Or "I know some people do not like the reforms because…."

E.g.

"I am aware that the Choose and Book system has been criticised because if patients can choose where they are treated it may lead to over-demand for some hospitals and under-demand for others. Hospitals with under-demand may then have to close which would reduce overall capacity in the NHS. If this does in fact happen then it is obviously an undesirable outcome."

Gender & cultural awareness

In the UK at present 60% of medical students are female. Do you think we should have equal quotas for medical school places for males and females?

"I think entry to medical school should be based on merit measured by objective factors such as exam results and interview performance and not on the basis of factors such as gender or race or any other factor which could be perceived as discriminatory. I'm not sure why female medical students currently outnumber male students but I don't see why it should cause any problems."

What do you think will be the consequences of having more female doctors than male doctors?

"In some cases and for certain conditions a patient may prefer to see a doctor of the same sex. However on the whole I can't see any major consequences being caused by there being more female doctors than male doctors since all doctors undergo the same training and are capable of treating patients to the same high professional standards."

Medicine will bring you into contact with a vast range of different people, with different cultures; what experience have you had of different types of people?

"At my [school/university/on my gap year/school exchange/holidays/travels] I had the opportunity to come into contact with people from different cultural backgrounds. However I prefer to think of people as individuals rather than on the basis of belonging to a different cultural group to my own. However I am aware of the fact that to avoid misunderstandings or causing offence it is sometimes necessary to be aware of differing beliefs and attitudes whether arising from cultural, religious or personal practices."

Issues involved in research

Is research important?
What's the point of research?

"Research is very important. Virtually all medical treatments which exist today are derived either directly or indirectly from research discoveries. Continuing research is necessary to improve existing treatments and to discover new ones and the underlying causes of illness."

Name some research?

Most medical schools have their own research programmes and it would be impressive if you could quote some of the research being done by the university which is interviewing you.

E.g.

"I was reading last week that St. George's University has won a grant of $19.7 from the Bill and Melinda Gates Foundation to develop an HIV vaccine that stimulates immune responses in the lining of the vagina, which serves as the entry point for HIV for most women."

Information such as this is easily found on university websites.

If a benefactor offered you a huge amount of money to set up a Medical Research Institute and invited you to become its director, what research area would you choose to look at, and why?

"The World Health Organisation (WHO) says Aids, tuberculosis (TB), measles, malaria, diarrhoeal diseases such as dysentery and cholera, and acute respiratory infections such as pneumonia are responsible for 90% of all deaths due to infectious diseases. Diarrhea alone contributes to the deaths of 2 million to 3 million young children each year so research funding could be best spent investigating solutions to problems like these"

What are the ethical issues involved in research?

- Does the research have genuine scientific value?

- Is the work original i.e. not plagiarised?

- Does the research require the approval of an ethics committee?

- Will the research involve animals? If so will their treatment follow acceptable standards?

- Will the research involve humans? If so issues to consider are:

- Has consent been obtained from the subjects?

- In order to obtain consent the purpose and what is involved in participation must be fully explained.

- Have any risks been fully explained?

- Will a placebo be used? Is it ethical to use a placebo on an ill person?

- Can a participant leave the trial without it negatively affecting their treatment?

- Have sufficient measures been taken to preserve the confidential data of the participants and preserve their anonymity?

- Will all the academics who worked on the research be given due credit in any published papers?

Answering Ethical Case Studies

Many med schools now include some kind of ethical case as part of the interview. This may take the form of a question posed to you in the interview or you may be given the case to work on before the interview and then be asked to present your conclusions to the interviewers.

In any kind of ethical case there will usually not be a "right" or "wrong" answer. The object is to discover if you are aware of the ethical issues involved and can apply them to a set of facts.

When answering a case study try and mention the perspective of all parties involved, patients, doctors, relatives and the courts. Look at the problem from all possible angles, generally the more things you mention the better.

Most of the ethical cases you will encounter at interview will fall into one of four categories –

- **Confidentiality**

- **Consent**

- **Resource Allocation**

- **End of Life**

Let's look at some of the issues you should be

aware of for each category and see how they can be applied to a particular scenario.

Confidentiality

Patients have a right to confidentiality and a right to expect that information about them will not be disclosed without their permission.

This right arises from two sources:

1. Doctors have a common law duty of confidentiality because the law recognises that it is in the public interest for patients to be able to trust their doctors to maintain confidentiality.

2. The GMC which regulates doctors states - "Patients have a right to expect that information about them will be held in confidence by their doctors. Confidentiality is central to trust between doctors and patients. Without assurances about confidentiality, patients may be reluctant to give doctors the information they need in order to provide good care."

Note: GMC guidance does not have the force of law although the courts consider its guidance persuasive. A doctor not following GMC guidance may be struck off the register.

However there are certain circumstances when a doctor can breach confidentiality and certain circumstances when they must breach confidentiality.

Some statutes **require** disclosure e.g. *Public Health (Control of Disease) Act 1984 and Public Health (Infectious Diseases) Regulations 1988.* A doctor must notify the relevant local authority officer (usually a public health consultant) if he suspects a patient of having a notifiable disease. AIDS and HIV are not notifiable diseases.

GMC guidance to doctors also **allows** (but there is no obligation to do so) disclosure of personal information without consent where failure to do so may expose the patient or others to risk of death or serious harm. However before making the disclosure a doctor must –

- Attempt to persuade the patient to inform the person first.

- If the patient refuses, inform the patient you are going to make the disclosure.

Note this guidance only allows disclosure to an identifiable person at risk, not a general disclosure.

Despite the common law duty of confidentiality the courts sometimes support doctors who feel they need to breach confidentiality –

E.g.

W v Edgell [1990] 1 ALL ER 835

The complainant was a patient in a secure hospital after killing five people. He applied to a mental health tribunal to be transferred to a regional unit. Dr Edgell a psychiatrist, was asked by W's lawyers to provide a confidential expert opinion to show that W was not a danger to the public. Unfortunately Dr Edgell believed that in fact W was still dangerous and knowing that his opinion would not be included in the patient's notes, sent a copy to the medical director of the hospital and to the Home Office.

W brought an action for breach of confidence.

The Court of Appeal held that the breach was justified in the public interest, however, the Court said the risk must be 'real, immediate and serious'.

Now let's see how we might apply these principles to a scenario –

Dan visits his GP who diagnoses him as suffering from syphilis. Dan admits to visiting a prostitute a few weeks previously. The GP suggests Dan tells his wife as she may need to come in for tests herself, the GP also knows that Dan's wife is 7 months pregnant. Dan refuses saying that the marriage has been going through a rough patch recently and if his wife found out he had visited a prostitute that he is sure she would ask for a divorce.

What should the GP do?

The issues to consider are

- Patient autonomy i.e. the principal that a doctor should respect his patients wishes and Dan does not want his wife told.

- Confidentiality, arising both from a legal duty of confidentiality and GMC guidance.

- Risks to Dan's wife if she is not informed she may be infected

- Risks to the baby

- Consequences to Dan if his wife finds out

Syphilis is not a notifiable disease, in any case the legislation only requires notification to a local authority officer and not anyone else such as Dan's wife so this does not help the GP.

The GP must weigh up the consequences to Dan of disclosing the information to his wife with the possible consequences to the wife and baby if he does not disclose. Although in law a foetus is not a person and has no rights until it is born.

Following GMC guidance since Dan's wife is an identifiable person and may be at risk of serious harm (contracting syphilis) the GP may breach confidentiality and inform her of her husbands condition. However before he does this he should try and persuade Dan to do it himself, explaining fully the possible risks to his wife and baby. He should explain to Dan that if he does not tell her himself that he will do it.

Consent

Cases involving consent usually fall into one of two categories

- A competent person refuses consent to a treatment

- An incompetent person refuses consent to a treatment

A patient must consent to any medical treatment otherwise the doctor commits a battery which is a criminal offence. Battery is any non-consensual touching - it does not have to harm the patient.

So a patient must be competent and consent.

Competence

Adults – to be competent must be 18 or over and satisfy the following conditions set out in the legal case of Re: C

- comprehend and retain treatment information

- believe it AND

- weigh it up to arrive at a choice

Children

16 and over are treated as adults and can consent (The Family Reform Act 1969)

Under 16 – may be able to consent if they are "Gillick" competent i.e. has sufficient intelligence and understanding to enable him / her to understand the treatment and implications of treatment.

So for example a doctor could prescribe contraception to an under 16 year old if he felt they were competent without informing the parents.

If a competent adult refuses treatment

The doctor must respect their wishes even if the patient will die (this also applies to pregnant women)

Per Lord Templeman in Sidaway v Board of Governors of Bethlem Royal Hospital [1985] 1 AC 171

"The patient is entitled to reject advice for reasons which are rational, or irrational, or for no reason."

If a competent child refuses treatment

Although a child is judged competent at 16 they are treated differently from adults and may not have the right to refuse treatment. A refusal of consent which would result in the death or permanent disability of the child may be overridden by a parent or the Court.

E.g.

Re M [1999] 2 FLR 1097

M was a competent 15 ? year old who required a heart transplant but refused consent on the grounds that she did not want someone else's heart. It was considered to be in her best interests to have the transplant.

If an adult refuses treatment for a child

If a parent refuses to consent to treatment for their child (e.g. a Jehovah's Witness refusing to allow a child to be given a blood transfusion) then doctors are permitted to treat the child without consent in order to avoid the death or permanent disability of the child.

If an incompetent adult refuses treatment

There are no statutes covering this except for patients detained under the Mental Health Act which only permits compulsory treatment in relation to the psychiatric condition for which the patient has been "sectioned".

For treatment for other conditions the GMC gives guidance that treatment may be given if it is in the patients "**best interest**".

Note that relatives etc cannot consent or refuse consent for another adult even if they are incompetent.

Example.

Sarah a 27 year old patient with severe learning difficulties has developed renal failure and requires dialysis while she is awaiting a kidney transplant. However she has recently become difficult and begun refusing dialysis as she does not like staying for long periods in the dialysis room.

Issues –

- Patient autonomy, the doctors should respect as far as possible Sarah's wishes

- Is Sarah competent? Can she comprehend and retain treatment information, believe it and weigh it up to arrive at a choice? (the Re: C test)

- Have doctors made sufficient effort to explain to Sarah the consequences of refusal of treatment?

- Have doctors sufficiently acknowledged Sarah's needs and addressed her dislike of staying in the dialysis room? What about providing entertainment e.g. TV / books while she has treatment?

- While doctors do not have to follow wishes of relatives they should try and take their opinions into account.

As it seems that Sarah is not competent the doctors would have to carefully weigh up whether it was in her best interest to treat her against her wishes. If they do not treat her she will die. On the other hand forcing her to have treatment on a regular basis against her will, which may involve restraining her or sedating her, may cause Sarah intolerable distress.

On balance treating her is probably the best solution but this case shows that there is often not a "right" answer and not treating her could equally be argued.

Resource allocation

Professional guidance

The GMC states that a doctor should consider the needs of his patients individually, whilst also taking into account that treatment for a particular patient may impact on the availability of treatment other patients and the community.

It also states that those whose healthcare needs are greatest or most urgent on clinical assessment should receive priority.

National Institute for Clinical Excellence (NICE)

Is a Special Health Authority for England and Wales. It is part of the National Health Service (NHS) and its stated role is to

"provide patients, health professionals and the public with authoritative, robust and reliable guidance on current 'best practice."

Health professionals have an obligation to provide treatment which NICE has recommended to be provided.

105

Legal Considerations

The European Convention on Human Rights

Article 2 states that there is a 'right to life'. However this does not impose an obligation on member states to fund every treatment, they may act reasonably in allocating limited resources.

A refusal to fund medical treatment because of the advanced age of the patient could be a breach of Article 2 and Article 14 (prohibition on discrimination).

Treatment in EU Member States under E112

Prior authorisation from the Department of Health can be obtained for a patient to receive treatment abroad under the E112 scheme where he/she would otherwise face 'undue delay'.

What is undue delay?

There is no clear cut answer, however in the case of **Watts v Bedford PCT and the Department of Health [2004] EWCA Civ 166** a patient was refused E112 treatment in France for a hip replacement since the waiting time of one year for her operation in the UK was considered normal. The court said the fact that a waiting time is normal (in the UK) does not necessarily mean that it is reasonable and that other factors need to be taken into account such as whether the patient is in pain, has had repeated delays in treatment or will suffer deterioration if treatment is delayed.

Judicial Review

A patient who has been refused treatment may appeal to the court by way of judicial review. This is a process whereby the courts will look at the WAY in which the decision to refuse treatment has been taken to ensure that correct procedures were followed relevant considerations taken into account and was it reasonable and proportionate.

They will not however get involved in deciding if the decision itself was correct.

In **R v Cambridge HA ex p B [1995] 2 All E.R. 129** the court refused to overturn the Health Authorities decision to not provide further treatment to a 10 year old girl with leukaemia saying –

"Difficult and agonising judgements have to be made as to how a limited budget is best allocated to the maximum advantage of the maximum number of patients. That is not a judgement which the court can make."

Let's try and apply the principles to a case –

You have one dialysis machine to share between three patients. One is a 17-year-old drug addict who has just overdosed, one is a 40-year old woman with terminal breast cancer and only 6 months of life expectancy, the third one is a 70-year old marathon runner. Who gets the machine?

There will be no right or wrong answer, but issues to discuss will include –

- Are any of them in more urgent need i.e. in more danger of dying sooner than the others? GMC guidance requires doctors to give priority to those whose needs are more urgent.

- Deciding to treat on the basis of the age of the patient may be illegal under Article 2 and Article 14 (prohibition on discrimination) of the European Convention of Human Rights.

- Is the treatment likely to be more successful on any particular patient?

- Should we take into account the fact that the 17-year-old has inflicted her condition on herself through abuse of drugs?

- Is she still using drugs? Will this affect the likely success of the dialysis and therefore whether she should be given dialysis?

- Should we try and measure a "value" of the treatment for each patient? For example –

  The 70 year old man, it may be tempting to think his remaining years of life are somehow worth less than a younger persons, but how is the enjoyment he gets from his remaining years and their intrinsic value measured? As mentioned this approach is probably also illegal.

  The 40 year old woman only has 6 months

left to live, it may seem a "waste" to give her the dialysis, but who can measure how valuable her last 6 months and the opportunity to say goodbye to her family etc are to her?

- How far should we respect patient autonomy i.e. if one patient insists they want treatment?

- Are all of them your patient? A doctor has a duty to act in the best interests of his patient, how far should he consider the needs of other patients elsewhere in the hospital?

End of life

General considerations:

Distinction between acts and omissions, there is a difference between actively killing someone and refraining from an action that may save or preserve them.

Doctrine of Double Effect, there is a moral distinction between acting with the intention to cause a person's death and performing an act where death is a foreseen but unintended consequence. E.g. providing high levels of pain relief but knowing that the pain relief may have the undesired consequence of hastening death.

The duty to act in the patient's best interest in some circumstances, if existing quality of life is so poor, then the balance of harms and benefits may indicate that continuing treatment is not a benefit to the patient.

Professional Guidelines

The BMA and GMC have both issued guidance suggesting that it is not an appropriate goal of medicine to prolong life at all costs, with no regard to its quality or the burdens of treatment and there is no ethical or legal obligation to provide it.

Also:

- There is no need to make a distinction between not starting the treatment and withdrawing it

- Oral nutrition and hydration (but not artificial) form part of a patient's basic care and should not be withdrawn

Legal considerations

It is illegal to actively assist in a suicide

A competent patient can refuse treatment, even if that results in the patient's death (***Re B Consent to treatment: Capacity, 2002***).

But a patient cannot request that a positive act is taken to end his/her life as this amounts to assisting a suicide.

Where the intention is to relieve pain, if the life of a terminally ill patient is shortened as a side effect of giving pain - relieving drugs, this is lawful under the doctrine of double effect.

Withdrawing or witholding treatment which results in the patient's death is permissible where it is not in the patient's interests to continue treatment, (***Airedale NHS Trust v Bland [1993] 1 All ER 821***).

Clinical case:

Baby A was born with severe brain damage and an inability to respond to stimuli. He needs artificial ventilation without which he would die almost immediately. The doctors believe it is not in the baby's best interests to continue with artificial ventilation. If ventilation is continued he would live for at most one year, probably experiencing pain and distress. The parents however believe the baby is getting better and refuse to agree to switch the ventilator off.

Issues to consider –

- Doctors must act in babies best interest

- Per guidance from GMC doctors do not have to prolong life at all costs

- Doctors cannot actively assist in killing the baby

- However withdrawing treatment is legal.

- Due weight should be given to the parents wishes, however the doctors are not obliged to continue treatment.

- Resource issues – consideration must be given to the fact that the baby is occupying a ventilator which may be needed for other babies. Doctors have a duty to consider the needs of other patients for scarce resources.

Advance Directives

Are a legally recognised document (or verbal statement) setting out how someone wishes to be treated in the future if they become incapable of expressing their wishes. E.g. a wish not to be resuscitated in the event of cardiac arrest.

In order to be valid an advance directive must

- Be made by a competent adult (18 and over).

- Be entered into voluntarily

- The individual must be sufficiently informed about the medical prognosis if the advance refusal is respected.

- Be applicable to the circumstances that arise.

Doctors must respect advance directives in keeping with the principles of patient autonomy and consent. However in cases of doubt they may need to consider –

Is the directive valid?

Does it apply to the circumstances of this case?

Is there any evidence the patient has revoked it or changed his mind?

If there is any doubt then guidance from the GMC states that there should be a presumption in favour of life and emergency treatment should be provided.

Questions You Should Ask

At the end of the interview you may be given the opportunity to ask some questions of your own.

In job interviews it is virtually compulsory to have some questions prepared about the job you will be doing or the company. However this is not a job interview, you are applying to be a student so the range of questions you can ask is limited.

For this reason I don't recommend asking questions just for the sake of asking a question. It is quite acceptable when asked if you have any questions to just say, *"No I think all my questions have already been answered thank you."*

Nevertheless if you want to ask a question and think your question is reasonably intelligent, then feel free to do so.

Here are a couple of questions which will always go down well –

If there has been a question in the interview you struggled with or were not sure if you gave the right answer it is always good to ask –

"When you asked me about....X.....what were you looking for in the answer?"

Even if you messed up the answer to the question this shows that you are aware of your weaknesses and show an interest in learning, which will no doubt impress the interviewers.

Another good question to pose is to ask the interviewers what THEY think the best things about their medical school are. This gives them a chance to boast a bit and again shows that you are interested in learning from THEM.

Finishing

After you have asked your questions the interviewers may end the interview themselves or may ask you if you want to say anything else. In either case thank the interviewers for seeing you and say it was nice to meet them. Shake their hands before you leave.

What If the Interview Was Unfair?

Occasionally it happens that someone feels that their interview wasn't fair, and sometimes (but not always) they are right.

There are usually four ways an interview could be unfair –

1. The interviewers were rude or made fun of you.

2. The questions asked were improper e.g. asking a female candidate if she plans to have children.

3. The interview was not in the format you were told.

4. The questions were too difficult.

Situations 1, 2 and 3 are easier to recognise. No one should have to put up with a rude or overly aggressive interviewer, nor is it acceptable for an interviewer to mock or laugh at a candidate or ask questions which are discriminatory in nature.

Similarly, the interview should be in the format you were told, it is not acceptable to spring surprises on you at the last minute.

Situation 3 is harder to recognise or prove, because

you may feel that a question was unfairly difficult but it would only be unfair if other candidates were not asked similar questions. The problem is how do you know what other candidates were asked?

In any case, if you feel strongly that your interview was unfair in any way, you should contact the university concerned as soon as possible after the interview to make your concerns known. There have been cases of people being given second interviews, so sometimes the universities will admit it if a mistake has been made.

Fortunately the vast majority of interviews are fair and well conducted so hopefully this is not a situation you will face.

Multiple Mini Interviews

Many medical schools have modified their admission interview process to include Multiple Mini-Interviews or MMIs. Rather than facing a single interview panel in a single sitting, candidates participate in a series of short mini-interview sessions that focus on a single question, task or scenario. MMI's include some traditional questions such as those elaborated earlier in this book. However, some MMI stations go beyond the straight forward interview questions to evaluate a wide range of skills and characteristics associated with successful doctors in context. Key skills examined include*:

1. critical thinking (organisational and problem solving skills)

2. ethical decision making

3. communication skills

4. insight and integrity (self-evaluation)

5. empathy

6. initiative and resilience

7. teamwork.

*Actual skills tested may vary from school to school, with the 7 skills above being the *most common skills listed on university web sites. A more comprehensive list garnered from university websites also includes: cultural competency, general knowledge of healthcare, general knowledge of the health delivery system and related issues, reliability, dependability, social and interpersonal skills, adaptability, work ethic and service orientation.*

Many mini-interviews, however, are highly participatory and may focus on a case study to be discussed with the interviewer or a scenario, skit, or collaboration in which the candidate engages with a *human simulator* - an actor trained to portray a character with whom you interact while the interviewer merely observes. Finally, MMIs may entail written tasks that candidates execute on a computer (with internet disabled). For those who are not computer buffs and in the event of problems, a computer technician is generally on hand to resolve technical difficulties that arise in the course of the written assignments.

MMI questions, cases, scenarios, skits and assignments do not focus on clinical skills or require advanced scientific or medical knowledge as this would give an unfair advantage to science students and health personnel. Instead, the questions and scenarios are drawn from real-life problems and professional and inter-personal situations which doctors and non-doctors may encounter on a daily basis.

MMI scenarios are designed to elicit a wide range

of approaches and responses. Sometimes an assignment, question or statement will be provided at the end of the scenario. This will help you to focus your thoughts and your argument.

WHY USE MMIs?

The MMI protocol is considered more psychometrically reliable than traditional interview processes. As individual performance varies substantially from task to task, evaluation that uses multiple discrete scenarios is considered a more efficient measure of student performance than a single extended interview.

MMIs tend to be more popular than traditional interviews amongst candidates and interviewers. Interviewers report that by repeatedly evaluating a single question/ scenario/skill set, they are more focused and can score and rank candidates more objectively. Candidates, on the other hand, appreciate having multiple opportunities for success. The pressure of "blowing" one short scenario or failing to establish rapport in one mini-interview is far less than the pressure of potentially undermining an entire panel interview. Candidates have the opportunity to start fresh each time they leave one room or cubicle and enter another. Furthermore, the focused questions and scenarios used in the MMIs can be viewed from multiple perspectives. This enables candidates, particularly candidates from diverse, non-medical backgrounds the opportunity to showcase their underlying personal strengths and reasoning.

NO RIGHT ANSWERS

As MMI's are based on multi-faceted, real-life situations, there are no right answers to the questions and no correct responses to the situations that you will encounter. The purpose of the mini-interview is to assess your ability to apply general knowledge and underlying ethics to issues relevant to the culture and society in which you will be practicing if you complete medical school and become a doctor. Emphasis is placed on your ability to think on your feet and to take action or articulate and defend personal opinions clearly in a variety of contexts. You are expected to respond thoughtfully and ethically to the underlying issues and situations presented in the MMI and, in the case of discussion sessions, to defend the ideas you put forth.

LOGISTICS OF THE MMIs

Although logistics will vary from school to school, MMIs are typically carried out in isolated rooms or cubicles, called stations, each with a different assigned question, task or scenario specific to that room. Candidates cycle from room to room on a precise schedule while interviewers, actors, and scenarios are stationary. The scenario/task for each room is posted on the door for that room, and an additional copy of the scenario is generally posted inside the room.

Mini-Multiple Interviews are, as the name implies, short sessions, generally between 5 and 10 minutes in duration. The number of stations or interviews varies from school to school, but you can expect to participate in 5 to 10 different stations. Specific details as to the logistics of the MMIs at any given university, including the duration and number of the mini-interviews, are readily available on the school's web site.

The student typically has a minute or two to read the scenario and consider the underlying issue. Some institutions allow students to jot down notes they may wish to take into the interview. Having considered the assignment, the student enters the room when signalled to do so to answer a single traditional panel interview question, engage in discussion, react to an actor or actors, or engage in a collaborative or written task.

Many institutions allow students to take longer to think about the assignment or to ask for a clarification of terms or limited explanation of the scenario once inside the room, but the additional time used on such preliminaries is deducted from overall time allotted to that MMI. At the end of the stipulated time, the mini-interview ends, and students move on to the next MMI. Again, it is a good idea to visit the website of any school where you plan to interview to learn about the specific MMI process, including the number and duration of MMIs for that school and the types of questions and scenarios you can expect.

RESCHEDULING AND SPECIAL REQUESTS

Most universities hold MMIs only once per year, and rescheduling, regardless of the reason, is generally not allowed. You should, nonetheless, contact your university if you are unable to attend MMIs for which you have registered. Requests for accommodation from candidates with special needs are generally welcome and are typically handled by the testing or physical therapy units of the university in question. Contact your university if you require accommodation.

RAPID ASSESSMENT

Candidates often find themselves wondering if they can really articulate themselves on a complex topic in a short mini-interview. The answer is "Yes."

Although the issues and situations you will encounter in the MMIs mimic the complexity of real life, each question or scenario focuses on a single dominant skill, and the questions and situations you encounter have been carefully designed and scripted to give you ample time to respond adequately. In the case of discussion-based MMI's, interviewers often have a set of probing, related questions to ask you.

SCORING AND FEEDBACK

Although criteria for evaluation are university specific, you will likely be evaluated based on your ability to grasp the underlying issue presented in the question, assignment or scenario posted outside the MMI room, articulate it, and propose or model realistic, ethical responses consistent with the characteristics of 'Tomorrow's Doctors' who 'must be capable of regularly taking responsibility for difficult decisions in situations of clinical complexity and uncertainty'.

Typically, interviewers and evaluators are directed to assess your communication skills including verbal and non-verbal communications and to evaluate the strength of your arguments and responses in order to determine your suitability for the medical profession. Most universities give candidates a single universal score for each mini-interview, based on a scale that ranks them from negative to positive, from 'unsatisfactory' to 'outstanding'. The scores from all of the sessions are then averaged for an overall score on the MMI.

Evaluators may or may not interact with you during the mini-interview, depending on the type of scenario being carried out. At no point, however, will evaluators discuss your performance or score on the MMI.

Evaluators may work with a standardised rating scale scoring candidates on a scale from 1 to 10 together with an overall impression of unsuitable, less suitable, satisfactory or above average. They may consider points such as the candidates -

Verbal and non-verbal communication skills
The organization, consistency and strengths of the arguments displayed
The applicant's suitability for the medical profession

THE LOWDOWN ON INTERVIEWERS, OBSERVERS, AND ACTORS

Perhaps the most uncanny and uncomfortable aspect of the MMI is not knowing what or whom you might encounter when you open the door to the interview room. You may have a single interviewer who poses an objective question such as those outlined previously in this book. Conversely, the interview may consist of a discussion session in which the interviewer asks assigned 'probing questions' or you might walk into a room with an interviewer and an observer, or with an actor or actors and an observer. Observers typically observe your body language and evaluate verbal and non-verbal cues as you interact with an actor. Unlike interviewers, they generally do not speak or otherwise interact with you, and this can seem just plain rude. Don't take it personally.

Actors are trained and work from a script to ensure that all candidates have the same basic experience. Some actors, like some people, can be difficult or may find themselves in difficult circumstances. The situations they face will have no easy solutions, and frequently all you can realistically do is to steadfastly walk them through their problem or help them to calm down and sort out their thinking.

7 SCENARIOS WITH ANALYSIS

The scenarios below address the 7 most common skills and competency areas identified earlier:

1. critical thinking (organisational and

problem solving skills)

2. ethical decision making

3. communication skills

4. insight and integrity (self-evaluation)

5. empathy

6. initiative and resilience

7. teamwork

Each scenario analyzed below is followed by an explanation of responses and behaviours evaluators would likely look for in a successful candidate. For purpose of analysis, key skills being examined are labelled, focus statements or questions are provided in bold and probing questions are listed when appropriate.

SKILL 1: CRITICAL THINKING
SCENARIO

A message that recently appeared on the worldwide web warned readers of the dangers of Red Dye #4, a widely used artificial colorant, as a cause of an epidemic of diabetes and colon cancers. The biological explanation provided was that, at body temperature, Red Dye #4 releases toxic gasses which turn into cyanotic acid, the main ingredient of many household cleaners and anti-freeze. Cyanotic acid, they argued, causes cellular narcosis. Clinically, Red Dye #4 poisoning was argued to be a cause of stomach cramps, dizziness and fainting, muscular pain and/or numbness, anxiety, jaundice, and blurred speech and vision. The authors further claim that Red Dye #4 has not been removed from the market because the food and drug industries have powerful lobbies in Congress. They quoted Dr Robert Blakemore, who said, "The ingredients over-stimulate the cells of the digestive system, causing cellular damage of varying degrees."

Critique this message, in terms of the strength of the arguments presented and their logical consistency. Your critique might include an indication of the issues that you would like to delve into further before assessing the validity of these claims.

POSSIBLE RESPONSES

Critical thinkers will be quick to see that the arguments presented in the scenario ultimately lack validity and consistency. The conclusions drawn are based on a 'message', not on a research study. Virtually anyone can post just about anything on the web; consequently all sources are suspect, and any undocumented statement is an unreliable statement by default. Simply stated, a 'message' on the worldwide web is not an adequate source. Furthermore, the subject is politicized and the authors are potentially biased. They believe the food and drug industries aren't playing fairly because they have the protection of Congress. It is logical to infer that this belief could lead them to exaggerate or fabricate their claims in retaliation.

You would certainly want to know more about the authors and the research supporting and disputing their claim before accepting the statement above as fact.

Similarly, you would want to know more about Dr Blakemore and his research and qualifications before accepting the validity of his statement. You may note that his comments sound rather vague and pseudo-scientific. Phrases like "over-stimulate the cells of the digestive system" sound less than professional and seem almost unrelated to the previous description of Red Dye 4's effects. Dr Blakemore and his statement seem unreliable, leading you to wonder who he is and what other doctors and nutritionists have to say about Red Dye #4.

Finally, claims that powerful lobbying by the food and drug administration accounts for Red Dye #4 still being on the market must also be substantiated or dismissed. People sometimes see political conspiracies where none exist, and you would want to know if that is or is not the case here.

On a whole, the message is unsubstantiated, inconsistent, and suspect. The scenario raises interesting issues, but you would need to conduct additional research before drawing any conclusions.

SKILL 2: ETHICAL DECISION MAKING SCENARIO

Dr. Jones recommends placebos in the form of herbal medicines to his patients. There is no scientific evidence or widely accepted theory to suggest that placebos work, and Dr. Jones doesn't believe they do. He recommends herbal medicine to people with mild, generalized symptoms such as fatigue, headaches, and muscle aches because he believes that they will do no harm, and will give patients reassurance.

Consider the ethical problems that Dr. Jones' behaviour might pose. Discuss these issues with the interviewer.

PROBING QUESTIONS EVALUATORS MIGHT ASK

1. What's wrong with the way Dr. Jones treats his patients? Why is that wrong?

2. Why do you think Dr. Jones prescribes placebos?

3. Can you see any circumstances under which recommending a placebo might be the appropriate action?

4. What action would you take regarding Dr. Jones?

POSSIBLE RESPONSES

Placebos have been used for centuries in clinical practice and are still commonly used in research. Furthermore, some supplements once thought to have only a placebo effect are now known to have therapeutic effects—both positive and negative.

The simple fact that Dr. Jones uses placebos, then, is not the central issue here.

The ethical issue underlying this case is that in prescribing treatments he reasonably believes to be ineffective, and by not telling his patients of his true opinion (thus maintaining the placebo effect and giving patients reassurance) Dr Jones is acting paternalistically. He is treating the patient as a parent would treat a child with growing pains or a phantom stomach ache. He is deceiving his patients into feeling like some progress is being or will be made, and he is insulting their intelligence in the process.

Although all models have their strengths and weaknesses, a relationship between colleagues who share a common goal (the patient's health) or a relationship between rational contractors (who agree on a contract leading to health) is considered a far healthier basis for interaction. Paternalistic practitioners violate the patient's autonomy of rights by withholding certain information. Many would argue that the doctor is not treating his patients like fully rational adults and that he is consequently acting unethically. Furthermore, if Dr Jones's patients were to become aware of the deception, they might come to doubt the honesty and usefulness of all doctors.

Paternalism is an outmoded model of the doctor/patient relationship. Its popularity lies in the fact that paternalism can be used to control the patient for his or her own good. Dr Jones reassures patients in the short term and does no real harm in the long term as long as his patients do not discover that he is tricking them into merely thinking they feel better.

Despite its limitations, paternalism is sometimes necessary – when patients are incompetent or when knowledge of a diagnosis would do more harm than good. Furthermore, deception such as that practiced by Dr Jones is necessary if we are to use placebos. Such deception might be allowable when it does no harm to the patient or to the reputation of the profession, and when there are potential benefits.

It is difficult to decide what action to take as Dr Jones' use of placebos does no harm and possibly some good is done. You could report Dr Jones to his or to your superiors, speak to him in private, or entirely overlook this transgression. Being relatively inexperienced, your reaction should be moderate; you should seek out more professional opinions on the matter before taking any action.

SKILL 3: COMMUNICATION SKILLS SCENARIO

You are a waiter at a restaurant. It is the dinner-hour rush, and you have an irate customer on your hands. She refused the first table you offered her and made several critical remarks about the ambiance, the service and your attire. As you are taking the customer's order she informs you that she intends to use a two-for-one coupon and to take the second meal home in a doggie-bag. Unfortunately, this is not allowed. The coupon applies only when two people dine. Furthermore, the coupon does not cover the cost of drinks or desserts (thus the restaurant still makes money on the second customer). Having seated the customer and brought her ice water and an appetizer, you must now explain that she cannot use the coupon to take a meal away.

Enter the room where you will find the customer.

SKILLS AND BEHAVIOURS EVALUATORS MAY LOOK FOR

1 Professionalism. Regardless of how difficult the customer is, your job is to wait on her professionally. You need not agree with her comments, but you should show you are listening by showing her the seating options, interacting with respect and refraining from responding to her caustic comments.

2 Concern. Even though the customer seems a difficult case, you need to listen to her without judging her. You may not agree with her comments or concerns, but you need not enter into a debate with her, critique or belittle her either.

3 A firm but fair attitude. Don't allow yourself to be drawn into the customer's negativity. Even though you have to tell the customer that she cannot use the coupon for take-away food, you can tell her that in a pleasant tone.

4   Consistency is probably preferable to compromise here. Your evaluators will likely be observing to see if you can diplomatically hold your position or if you give in to the irate customer. Remember, you are a waiter, and only a manager can approve an exception to the policy.

5   Collaboration. At some point towards the end of the interview, you may need to tell the customer that you will have to call on a manager to resolve the issue. The scenario does not mention a manager, but it is reasonable to assume that one would be on hand during rush hour. It is important to show initiative in the scenarios, but it is just as important to know when to ask for help.

6   Effective body language. Actions often speak louder than words, and evaluators will likely watch for subtle physical clues you express while interacting with the customer. Avoid bristling up, crossing your arms, tapping your fingers or feet, glaring at the customer in disbelief or otherwise showing frustration.

SKILL 4: INSIGHT & INTEGRITY (SELF-EVALUATION)
SCENARIO

You are just completing your first year of medical school. Your school has a peer professionalism program that requires that your colleagues assess you. You also assess yourself. The findings of these evaluations have been collated below, along with data reflecting the class mean performance.

Behaviour	Score by Self	Score by Peers	Class Mean (N=150)
Takes on extra work to help colleagues	5.0	4.4	4.8
Encourages communication and collaboration among colleagues	4.0	4.5	4.5
Manages conflict in a collegial and respectful manner	4.0	3.5	4.5
Displays empathy towards patients appropriately	4.0	3.8	4.8
Listens and responds respectfully to others	5.0	4.8	4.2
Acknowledges limits on own knowledge and responsibility	4.0	4.4	4.6

Discuss your evaluation with the interviewer.

PROBING QUESTIONS EVALUATORS MAY ASK

1 Comment on the adequacy and limitations of peer- and self-evaluations.

2 Based on the results, what do you consider to be your strengths? Your weaknesses?

3   Comment on the difference in how you see yourself and how others see you.

4   What opportunities for professional development do you see in this evaluation? What threats to professional development do you see?

5   What other information might you use to assess your professional development?

6   Do you have additional comments before we end the discussion?

POSSIBLE RESPONSES

Peer and self-evaluations are certainly subjective and prone to bias. The fact remains, however, that such evaluations give valuable insights into how you perceive yourself and how others perceive you. Such perceptions can become self-fulfilling prophecies (positive and negative), on the one hand, and they give valuable insights as to your actual performance on the other. Despite their subjectivity, peer and self-evaluations must be taken seriously as a PART of your overall evaluation.

Your strengths would tend to be those behaviours where you and your peers rank you above the class average, in this case: 'Listens and responds respectfully to others' where you give yourself a perfect 5.0 score and your peers give you a cumulative score of 4.8. The class average for this skill is 4.2. Other than this, though, you have no outstanding strengths and perform at or below the class average on all other skills according to your own and/or your peers' assessments. Your weaknesses would clearly be your difficulty managing conflict in a collegial and respectful manner and your ability to display empathy towards patients appropriately. It is worth noting that generally you have a significantly more positive perception of your performance/skills than your peers do.

Your ratings, considered in light of class averages, suggest you have difficulty interacting with others when the situation demands advanced inter-personal skills. You can improve across the board but most especially in terms of your ability to manage conflict in a collegial and respectful manner and your ability to display empathy appropriately.

The best thing about this evaluation is that there is ample opportunity for improvement. Your evaluation suggests that you need to rethink your professional interactions and to establish clear goals for improvement and indicators of progress in this area so that you can ensure that you make progress. Clearly you listen and respond respectfully (passive behaviour), but at the same time, you run into problems when it comes to interactions, particularly if when it comes to managing conflict and your emotions. Having noted these weaknesses, you now have the opportunity to work on interpersonal interactions. Your self-rating of 'Acknowledges limits based on your own knowledge and responsibility' would be a good starting point. Clearly you struggle with professional boundaries, possibly explaining why you have difficulty managing conflict and displaying empathy.

The main threat here is likely your insecurity about your ability to set and work within limits. If you are comfortable with you boundaries, you will likely be more confident and skilful in your reactions to different situations. With more confidence (that you are acting within your limits) your ability to manage conflict and show empathy should improve. If, on the other hand, you do not address this underlying issue your professional performance is likely to decline as the demands on you increase as you progress through your program.

As noted, self- and peer-evaluations are subjective and should be used in conjunction with other performance indicators. These findings should certainly be reviewed in the context of your grades, evaluations from faculty and supervisors and, if possible, feedback from patients.

SKILL 5: EMPATHY
SCENARIO

Your work needs you and a co-worker (John, a colleague from another branch of the company) to represent your company at a trade fair in the Florida cays. You and John have travelled by air to Florida but now need to take a boat to the remote cay where the trade fair is being held. You have just arrived at the pier.

Enter the room. John is in the room*.

*Here you will be interacting with an actor playing the part of John while an observer evaluates you.

BACKGROUND**

**In a SKIT the actor will reveal this information as part of the 'act'. You will not be given written background.

John, whose son drowned 6 months ago, discovers upon arriving at the pier that he is very anxious about travelling by water. This is John's first encounter with water since the accident and presumably latent feelings about his son's death are surfacing. John had not experienced anxiety travelling by water in the past, but now he is gripped with fear that the boat will capsize and everyone will drown.

Inside you will find John waiting for you.

SKILLS AND BEHAVIOURS EVALUATORS MAY LOOK FOR

1. Listens well.

2. Expresses empathy without patronizing.

3. Avoids making light of John's concerns.

4. Normalizes concerns, noting that feelings of anxiety are common and manageable.

5. Models positive behaviours that may help John to feel less anxiety.

6. Helps John to explore his alternatives and evaluate their effectiveness.

7. Helps John separate reality (low risk) from the emotional response of anxiety.

8. Remains supportive regardless of John's decision to get on the boat or not.

SKILL 6: INITIATIVE AND RESILIENCE SCENARIO

Your workplace has acquired a much needed bulk printer, and most staff attended a basic training session to learn how to use and maintain the machine. You, however, are a recent hire, and did not participate in the training. You know your way around a printer, and a few weeks after starting your new job, you are changing the ink when the cartridge explodes and leaks over the drum, effectively costing your company thousands in repairs. A secretary sees this happen and immediately calls to report the accident to your supervisor. She tells you the supervisor is expecting you to report immediately.

What issues contribute to or compromise your ability to take the initiative and show resilience in this scenario?

PROBING QUESTIONS AN EXAMINER MIGHT ASK

1. What basic questions about initiative and resilience does the scenario raise?

2. How would you react if called on to perform a non-life threatening medical procedure you have not been trained to carry out?

3. Are people obligated to do the right thing even when doing so is against their best interests?

4. To what extent is your workplace responsible for the accident?

WHAT MARKERS WILL LIKELY BE LOOKING FOR

You take the initiative to change the ink even though you have not been trained in the proper use and maintenance of the bulk copier. It may well be that the packaging on the ink was faulty, but because you acted without training it is highly probable that you will be blamed for the accident. Whether or not you believe you are responsible for the ink spill, you must admit that you are responsible for acting beyond the scope of your training – for assuming you are competent. This is why it is important to follow established procedures, know your limitations and follow protocol whether you perceive it to be necessary or not. Failing to do so creates confusion and complications.

Once the ink has spilled, you are essentially robbed of your initiative by the over anxious secretary who leaps to the phone to report you. Although you may wish to talk to her, explaining you wish you had had the opportunity to report on your own, you should not blame her or otherwise comment on her behaviour at this point. Complaining to or about the secretary would suggest that you are unwilling to face the problem you created. The first issue you must address is the damaged copier. You have not been robbed of your resilience, and can demonstrate this by going to see your boss promptly and professionally regardless of how you might feel about the secretary who reported you.

As a medical student you must be guided by professional ethics and common sense when it comes to taking the initiative in an emergency. You do not yet have the training or obligations of a doctor. Your first course of action must be to get the victim the professional attention he or she needs. In the event that is not possible, you should be guided by the precept that the 'cure', even if it causes damage, must do more good than harm. In taking the initiative to render assistance beyond your training you must weigh your options (worst case scenario if you do and worst case scenario if you don't take action) and calculate your odds of a successful intervention. The more extreme (life threatening) the emergency, the farther you may consider going with your intervention, but bear in mind that legally and ethically you are more like a lay person than a doctor. In no case should you, a student, perform a procedure that has a high risk of harming or killing the patient.

The majority of people doing the right thing the majority of the time is the oil that greases society and keeps it running smoothly. Furthermore, doctors take specific oaths committing themselves to ethical behaviours, and these guide their actions and interactions. Doing the right thing, however, is an endless task, and doctors must balance the obligation to do the right thing with the obligation to take good care of yourself.

Although your workplace failed to train you, you are ultimately responsible for the damage done to the copier: you knew you were not trained and still decided to change the ink, putting yourself in a very vulnerable position. Although you may mention your previous experience with copiers and the fact that the ink cartridge may have been defective, your boss will certainly wonder why you didn't ask someone with training (such as the over-anxious secretary) to change the ink. Again, your choice to act beyond the scope of your training when doing so is clearly not required is a key factor here.

SKILL 7: TEAMWORK
SCENARIO

A variety of items that are not extremely valuable have gone missing from your dorm room over the last few months. Nothing of yours, however, has gone missing, leading your frustrated roommates to suspect that you are the culprit. To clear the air and hopefully put an end to the thefts you call a meeting with your roommates.

How will you conduct the meeting?

BEHAVIOURS AND SKILLS THE EVALUATOR MAY BE LOOKING FOR

1. Establishes an atmosphere of honesty and intellectual curiosity.

2. Sets a common goal (not to clear your name but to solve the mystery, stop the thefts).

3. Clarifies the goal and establishes a workable process for the meeting.

4. Is open to a wide variety of theories and analyzes them objectively (including the theory that you are the thief).

5. Listens respectfully and encourages others to do the same.

6. Remains impartial, non-judgmental, un-biased.

7. Recognizes and validates students' contributions and concerns.

8. Stays organized under pressure.

9. Summarizes findings and seeks a consensus of opinion before moving on.

10. Seeks to effectively distinguish between fact and speculation.

11. Differentiates between corroborated and circumstantial evidence.

12. Closes meeting with a summary of what was accomplished, including an agreed upon strategy for moving forward if appropriate.

7 ADDITIONAL MMI TOPICS FOR PRACTICE

1 CRITICAL THINKING SCENARIO

Universities in developing countries are commonly faced with the complicated task of balancing the educational needs of their students with the available pool of qualified faculty. As a result, classes are often taught by faculty who lack the qualifications and/or experience to teach them. The only alternative is to wait until suitable faculty become available to teach advanced courses, but doing so would dramatically impede students' academic progress and lead to high levels of attrition. This, in turn, would result in a lack of graduates and doctors in the country. Some argue that developing countries must work with the resources they have, while others argue that a substandard education leads to substandard doctors and this simply cannot be tolerated.

Discuss the issues raised with the examiner.

2 ETHICAL DECISION MAKING
SCENARIO

One of your friends calls you telling you that she has been wrongfully arrested and needs someone to post her bail. You arrive at the police station to discover that your friend was participating in a peaceful protest that turned violent when protestors and police clashed. Your friend says she was arrested simply for being in the wrong place at the wrong time and did not take part in the violence, but the police tell you they have evidence that she was actively involved in the violence against police. To release your friend, you have to pay a bond $5,000.

Will you post bail for your friend? What basic precepts guide your decision?

3 COMMUNICATION SKILLS
SCENARIO

You and a colleague are on a conference call with a long-winded, tedious client who has a heavy accent. As the call goes on and on, your colleague starts mocking the client's accent and making snide comments about the client to you. As your conversation with your colleague is muted so the client can't hear what you say, you join in with a few disparaging comments of your own. A couple of hours later, you are called to an urgent meeting with your boss.

It seems that your side of the conversation was not muted, and the client heard everything you said even though you thought your colleague had muted the microphone. The client has called your boss and is threatening to fire your firm unless he receives an explanation and apology. Your boss demands that you write to the client in an effort to save the account.

Write the letter your boss demands.

4 INSIGHT AND INTEGRITY
SCENARIO

You are a student participating in a medical mission to a third world country where you are given the opportunity to observe doctors in clinical contexts. On a whole, you feel the mission is poorly organized and under supervised. Students are allowed to carry out medical procedures such as giving injections, flushing ear canals, suturing, and dressing wounds. Several students are taking advantage of the situation and passing themselves off as doctors with unwitting local patients. When you bring up these issues in a group meeting with your peers and supervisors, you are ridiculed for being 'uptight' and told to 'go with the flow'.

What would you do next?

5 EMPATHY
SCENARIO

Your college roommate comes to you frustrated with her progress in chemistry class. Although she did well in high school chemistry, she is finding college chemistry very difficult. To make matters worse, she recently found out that her parents are divorcing. This comes as a huge shock, and she feels that all things considered, perhaps she should quit school and go home.

Enter the interview room where you will find your roommate.

6 INITIATIVE AND RESILIENCE
SCENARIO

You are a member of a technical team charged by the mayor with analyzing deficiencies in the service delivery system at the local municipal hospital. You are presenting the report to the mayor and town council when it becomes apparent that one of the team members made a subtle but critical error in his section of the report. The mayor launches into a tirade blaming you for this mistake and accusing you of being professionally incompetent.

How will you respond to the mayor's accusations?

7 TEAMWORK
SCENARIO

Sophie is a mature engineering student who works in a civil engineering firm. She likes working with her hands and enjoys her technical and engineering classes. However, she has a marketing class that she finds difficult. The instructor has formed permanent class teams with weekly case studies to present to the class and a final team project to complete. Sophie fears she will have a difficult time attending group meetings and managing her responsibilities at work, and she feels she can complete the case study assignments and make presentations more efficiently on her own. She also dislikes relying on others for a final grade and gets frustrated trying to keep the team members focused on their tasks. Based on past experiences, Sophie fears that members will skip meetings, won't do their share of the work, or will have personality conflicts that lower everyone's grades. Sophie decides to go talk to her teacher in hopes of being allowed to complete the case study assignments and make presentations on her own. You are Sophie's teacher.

Enter the interview room where you will find Sophie waiting for you.

PREPARING FOR A SUCCESSFUL MMI

MMIs differ substantially from standard medical school interviews and require a unique approach in terms of preparation.

Besides the lists of skill areas to be examined,

most universities provide sample questions you can use to guide your preparation and orient you the general type and complexity of the questions scenarios and assignments you will encounter.

However, it makes little sense to memorize particular questions. Focus, instead, on developing your ability to:

- recognize the underlying skill or characteristic being examined in each MMI

- formulate a logical, thorough response within strict time limits

- interact and communicate effectively verbally, non-verbally (body-language), and in writing

- react thoughtfully and ethically to a wide range of issues

- think on your feet and respond genuinely, ethically, empathetically to a wide range of people and situations

- perform under pressure, moderate your anxiety, pace yourself

DEVELOP GENERAL KNOWLEDGE

Although the scenarios you encounter may not involve medical issues, familiarity with bioethics can be helpful in understanding the approach to ethical issues and decision making in general.

(The General Medical Council provides links to many free, online documents guiding the medical profession: *http://www.medicalcouncil.ie/News-and-Publications/Publications/Professional-Conduct-Ethics*)

You can also benefit by familiarizing yourself with current events and policy issues. Doing so hones your ability to understand the health delivery system and its challenges, to isolate the various sides of a problem, and to weigh the costs and benefits of a particular approach.

To prepare for stations involving skits and actors, start by recalling times you have interacted with people in (or yourself have been in) difficult or demanding situations. Analyze the situation and outcomes. Are you satisfied with your performance, or, in retrospect, would you do things differently? Consider the steps you would take when interacting with a friend (an enemy, a colleague, or a stranger) facing a difficult choice or situation. What would your goal be? What questions would you ask? What tone would you use? Would you give advice? In general, what is required for effective communication?

LISTEN CAREFULLY

MMI questions and scenarios are generally designed to ensure that you have carefully considered all sides of an issue in developing your position. Interviewers often ask probing questions designed to focus and direct the discussion. Similarly, actors provide subtle clues through their dialogue, actions and reactions to guide you. Listen carefully to everything the interviewer and actors say and pay attention to what actors say and do, focusing on the key question or issue being raised and taking advantage of any new information that may be introduced. Be prepared to change gears/positions/strategies in the course of the MMI if asked to do so or if your interactions with the actor seem ineffectual.

PRACTICE UNDER PRESSURE

A central challenge of MMIs is the strict time limit for each station. Practice answering questions within strict time limits. Many candidates find it challenging to speak on a focused topic for 5 to 10 minutes while others are just getting warmed up as the MMI ends. Record yourself if possible so that you can hear (and possibly see) yourself as the interviewer or observer will see you. If you have a dramatic colleague, friend or relative, enlist some help in acting out skits within tight timeframes. Do a post-mortem on the skit to determine if you came across as you intended. Make a video if possible and carefully analyze your body language.

SHOCKS AND SURPRISES

In the course of their work doctors are likely to encounter a wide range of unfamiliar personalities and situations, making flexibility a highly valued quality. Some MMIs are designed to push you out of your comfort zone and see how you react – tests of resilience, as it were.

In the course of your MMIs you may encounter:

- Examiners who deliberately appear uninterested in or bored with what you are saying. This is to test your communication skills and empathy and to see if you notice and attempt to re-engage the listener or if you seem not to notice or just plough on without addressing the situation.

- The presence of a third person sitting in the corner who doesn't say anything – this is an observer who will evaluate (grade) your performance while you interact with the other examiner or the actor(s).

- When you stop talking the examiner may just sit in silence without speaking or otherwise responding to you, this is probably just because they have standard instructions not to interact with students in order to keep the whole process objective. Alternatively the interview may conclude and you may be asked to leave the room. In that case a waiting area will be provided. Do not talk with other candidates you may encounter in the waiting area. Focus, instead, on calming and clearing you mind and reenergizing yourself for the remaining MMIs.

- In stations which have an actor playing a role, the actor may have been told to get angry with you. Other actors may get increasingly anxietal as you attempt to calm them down. You should be prepared for this, but should recognise that if the actor becomes angry it is probably because he or she feels you weren't sympathetic or understanding enough or that your attempts are misguided and ineffectual. You should, of course, try to address this.

As you reach each MMI station, read the directions and trust in the process and in yourself. Your interviewer, observer and actor(s) are highly trained, and the questions and scenarios are carefully designed to be addressed within the timeframe provided. Bear in mind, that whatever constraints, peculiarities or challenging personalities you meet in the interview rooms, all candidates get an experience nearly identical to yours. No one knows what they will encounter when they open the door. Successful candidates are those who focus on the question or scenario rather than worrying about what is on the other side of the door.

Note that at most universities, interviewers are allowed to clarify terms and instructions if the applicant is uncertain. If in doubt, ask for clarification.

Full List of 153 Questions

Complete list of 153 questions as reported by actual candidates from interviews organized by the following categories –

A - Knowledge of the Medical School
B - Motivation for medicine
C - Depth and breadth of interest
D - Team work
E - Personal Insight
F - Understanding of the role of medicine in society
G - Work Experience
H - Tolerance of ambiguity

A - Knowledge of the Medical School

1. What interests you about the curriculum at [Medical School]? What previous experiences have you had of learning in a small group setting?

2. When you read the [Medical School] prospectus, what appealed to you or interested you in the course here?

3. Tell us what attracts you most and least about [Medical School].

4. What do you know about the course at [Medical School]? Why do you think it will suit you personally?

5. What do you know about PBL? Why do you want to come to a PBL medical school?

6. What do you think are the advantages and disadvantages of a PBL course?

7. I expect you have thought about problem-based learning. Why do you think a PBL course will suit you personally?

8. What do you think are the advantages and disadvantages of coming to a new medical school?

9. This course will require a good deal of independent study, how have you managed this approach to learning in the past?

10. Why do you think problem based learning will suit you personally?

11. What previous experiences have you had of learning in a small group setting?

B - Motivation for medicine

1. Why do you want to be a doctor? What do you want to achieve in medicine?

2. What have you read or experienced in order to prepare you for medicine?

3. Why do you believe you have the ability to undertake the study and work involved?

4. Why do you want to be a doctor, rather than another profession that is caring or intellectually challenging?

5. What do you think being a doctor entails, apart from treating patients?

6. What branch of medicine do you think would interest you? Why?

7. When you think about becoming a doctor, what do you look forward to most and least?

8. What impact do you hope to make in the field of medicine?

9. What one question would you ask if you were interviewing others to study medicine? What would you most like us to ask you in this interview?

10. Why study medicine rather than any other health care profession? How do you think medicine differs from other health professions?

11. What aspect of healthcare attracts you to medicine?

12. Why do you want to be a doctor? If you were to become a doctor, how would you

wish your patients to describe you and why?

13. What steps have you taken to try to find out whether you really do want to become a doctor?

14. What things do you think might make people inclined to drop out of medical training?

15. There are many different ways of helping people. Why do you want to study medicine, rather than working in any other health or social care professions?

16. Can you tell us about any particular life experiences that you think may help or hinder you in a career in medicine?

17. How would you dissuade someone from going into Medicine.

18. How old are you when you become a consultant?

C - Depth and breadth of interest

1. Do you read any medical publications?

2. Tell us about Hippocrates.

3. Can you tell me about a significant recent advance in medicine or science? Why has this interested you?

4. What do you consider to be important advances in medicine over the last 50 / 100 years?

5. Can you tell us about any significant medical stories in the media at the moment?

6. Tell us about something in the history of medicine that interests you.

7. Have you seen a film or read a book recently that has made you think, and why?

8. What do you think is the most important medical discovery in the last 100 - 200 years, and why?

9. If a benefactor offered you a huge amount of money to set up a Medical Research Institute and invited you to become its director, what research area would you choose to look at, and why?

10. Can you tell us about a book or a film that has influenced you as a person or made you think, and why?

11. Tell me about someone who has been a major influence on you as a person / in your life?

12. What do you think was the greatest public health advance of the twentieth century?

13. Can you describe an interesting place you

have been to (not necessarily medical) and explain why it was so?

14. Do you think putting a man on the moon money well spent? If yes - why? If no - how would you have spent that money?

15. Tell me about a non-academic project or piece of organisation that you were involved in. How did it go?

16. If you had to have a gap year, and could go anywhere in the world or do anything, what would you chose to do, and why?

17. How do you think the rise in information technology has influenced / will influence the practice of medicine?

D - Team work

1. Thinking about your membership of a team (in a work, sport, school or other setting), can you tell us about the most important contributions you made to the team?

2. Can you think of a team situation where your communication skills have been vital? Tell us about the situation and your contribution.

3. Tell us about a group activity you have organised. What went well and what went badly? What did you learn from it?

4. Tell us about a team situation you have experienced. What did you learn about yourself and about successful team-working?

5. When you think about yourself working as a doctor, who do you think will be the most important people in the team you will be working with?

6. Who are the important members of a multi-disciplinary healthcare team? Why?

7. Are you a leader or a follower?

8. What are the advantages and disadvantages of being in a team? Do teams need leaders?

9. Modern day health care is very much a team effort. Please tell us a role that you have played in a team, and what you think you contributed.

10. What do you think of nurses developing extended roles and undertaking tasks previously done by doctors?

11. What do you think are the advantages and disadvantages of nurses replacing doctors as the first contact person in primary care?

12. When you are a doctor you will be working in a team. Who do you see as the key members of your team, and why? How will you help the team to develop?

E - Personal Insight

1. What ways of working and studying have you developed that you think will assist you through medical school? What will you need to improve?

2. How do you think you will cope with criticism from colleagues or other health professionals?

3. Give us an example of something about which you used to hold strong opinions, but have had to change your mind. What made you change? What do you think now?

4. Have you ever been in a situation where you realise afterwards that what you said or did was wrong? What did you do about it? What should you have done?

5. How do you think you will avoid problems of keeping up to date during a long career?

6. What are your outside interests and hobbies? How do these compliment you as a person? Which do you think you will continue at university?

7. Tell us two personal qualities you have which would make you a good doctor, and two personal shortcomings which you think you would like to overcome as you become doctor?

8. Medical training is long and being a doctor can be stressful. Some doctors who qualify never practice. What makes you think you will stick to it?

9. What do you think will be the most difficult things you might encounter during your training? How will you deal with them?

10. What relevance to medicine are the 'A' levels (apart from biology and chemistry) that you have been studying?

11. What skills do you think are needed in order to communicate with your patients; how do you think they are best acquired?

12. Can you learn communication skills?

13. How have you developed your communication skills?

14. What interests do you bring from school/ college life that you think will contribute to your studies and practice?

15. What challenges do you think a career in medicine will bring you?

16. What do you think you will be the positive aspects and the negative aspects of being a doctor? How will you handle these?

17. What attributes are necessary in a good doctor? Which do you have, and which do

you need to develop further?

18. Can you tell us about an interesting experience, and what you learned from it about yourself?

19. Thinking about yourself: what characteristics do you think you would most need to change in the course of becoming a good doctor?

20. If you could only tell me one thing about yourself, to help me to get a sense of you as a person, what would it be and why?

21. If you could change two things about yourself, what would they be and why?

22. What do you think are your priorities in your own personal development?

23. What qualities do you lack that would be useful for a doctor, and what do you intend to do about this?

24. What qualities do you think other people value in you?

25. How do you think other people would describe you?

26. How will you cope with being criticised or even sued?

F - Understanding of the role of medicine in society

1. What is wrong with the NHS?

2. What problems are there in the NHS other than the lack if funding?

3. What relevance has the Hippocrates oath to modern-day medicine?

4. What would you prefer in a doctor? Bad communication skills with good clinical skills or good communication skills with bad clinical skills? Why?

5. Would you argue that medicine is a science or an art, and why?

6. How do politics influence health care provision? Is it inevitable?

7. Why do you think we hear so much about doctors and the NHS in the media today?

8. Do you think doctors should set a good example to their patients in their own lives? How or why might this be difficult?

9. In what ways do you think doctors can promote good health, other than direct treatment of illness?

10. Do you think doctors and the NHS get a bad press, and if so, why?

11. From what you have read and found out, where do you see the health service going?

12. What are the arguments for and against non-essential surgery being available on the NHS?

13. What does the current government see as the national priorities in health care? Do you agree with these?

14. How should the health service achieve a balance between promoting good health, and in treating ill health?

15. What do you think are the similarities and differences between being a doctor today and being a doctor 50 years ago?

16. Should doctors have a role in regulating contact sports, such as boxing?

17. Do you think doctors should ever strike?

18. Do you think patient's treatments should be limited by the NHS budget or do they have the right to new therapies no matter what the cost?

19. What does the term 'inequalities in health' mean to you?

20. Do you think medicine should be more about changing behaviour to prevent disease or treating existing disease?

21. What do you think is the purpose of the health service in the 21st century?

22. What do you think are the chief difficulties faced by doctors in their work?

23. Why do you think people in the north of England live, on average, 5 years less than those in the south? Do you think this should be a matter for government intervention?

24. What are the arguments for and against people paying for their own health care as and when they need it?

25. What do you understand by the term 'holistic' medicine? Do you think it falls within the remit of the NHS?

26. How accurately do you think the media (particularly television) tend to portray the role of the doctor?

27. Do you think the bulk of medical treatment takes place in hospital or in the community? What makes you think this?

28. What do you think about the way doctors are shown in the media, say in the Simpsons or on the news? How do you think this will affect patients' views of their own doctors?

29. What do you think is the greatest threat to the health of the British population today?

30. Imagine you are on committee able to

recommend only one of two new surgical treatments to be made available through the NHS. The treatments are: an artificial heart for babies born with heart defects, or a permanent replacement hip for people with severe arthritis. Both treatments are permanent, ie never need repeating, and are of equal cost. On what grounds would you make your arguments?

31. Ten years ago most doctors in hospitals wore white coats; now few do. Why do you think this is? What do you think are the arguments for and against white coats?

32. Animals that are thought to be suffering are 'put down'. Should human suffering be treated in the same way?

33. Do you think more doctors or more nurses would be of greatest benefit to the nation's health?

34. What are the arguments for and against banning the sale of tobacco?

35. In the UK at present 60% of medical students are female. Do you think we should have equal quotas for medical school places for males and females? What do you think will be the consequences of having more female doctors than male doctors?

36. What issues should be considered in

deciding to terminate or not continue a patient's life-sustaining treatment?

37. Medicine will bring you into contact with a vast range of different people, with different cultures; what experience have you had of different types of people?

G - Work Experience

1. What experiences have given you insight into the world of medicine? What have you learnt from these?

2. What aspect of your work experience did you find the most challenging, and why?

3. In your work experience, what skills have you learnt that you can apply to medicine?

4. Can you give me an example of how you coped with a conflict with a colleague or friend; what strategy did you use and why?

5. Reflect on what you have seen of hospitals or a health care environment. What would you most like to organise differently, and why?

6. What aspect of your work experience would you recommend to a friend thinking about medicine, and why?

7. What impressed you most about the doctors in your work experience?

8. Can you think of a situation where good communication has saved the day and give a reason why?

9. Thinking of your work experience, can you tell me about a difficult situation you have dealt with and what you learned from it?

10. Have you visited any friends or family in hospital, or had work experience in a hospital? From these experiences, what did you see that you would like to change?

11. Can you tell me the key things you learned from your work experience, in caring or other settings?

12. What have you done on work experience/ in employment previously? What would you change about what you saw, if you could, and how would you set about this?

13. What do you think would be the advantages, and difficulties, for a person with a major physical disability (e.g. blindness) wishing to become a doctor?

14. Tell me about a project, or work experience, that you have organised, and what you learned from it?

H - Tolerance of ambiguity

1. Is it better to give health care or aid to impoverished countries? What do you

think about the activities of the charity Medecins sans Frontieres?

2. Do you think we should find out more about patients' views of their doctors, their illness or their treatments? How would you set about this?

3. What do you think are the major sorts of problems facing a person with a long-term health problem, such as difficulty breathing?

4. Why do you think it is that we cannot give a guarantee that a medical or surgical procedure will be successful?

5. What are the differences between length of life and quality of life?

6. Should alternative or complimentary medicine be funded by the NHS, and why?

7. Should the NHS be involved in non-essential surgery?

8. Should the NHS fund the treatment of self-inflicted diseases?

9. How do you think doctors should treat injury or illness due to self-harm, smoking or excess alcohol consumption?

10. Female infertility treatment is expensive, has a very low success rate and is even less

successful in smokers. To whom do you think it should be available?

11. Would you prescribe the oral contraceptive pill to a 14-year old girl who is sleeping with her boyfriend?

12. What is your feeling about euthanasia?

13. Would you perform abortions as a doctor? Under what conditions?

14. Is it right that Viagra should only be available to certain groups of men?

15. What do you think about the use of animals for testing new drugs?

16. How do you respond and what do you feel when you see a beggar in the street?

17. You have one liver available for transplant, but two patients with equal medical need. One is an ex-alcoholic mother with two young children, the other a 13 year old with an inborn liver abnormality. How would you decide to whom it should be given?

18. You have one dialysis machine to share between three patients with equal medical need. One is a 17-year-old drug addict who has just overdosed, one is a 40-year old woman with terminal breast cancer and only 6 months of life expectancy, the third one is a 70-year old marathon runner. Who gets the machine?

BEST OF LUCK!

Best of luck to everyone, I'd love to hear both your success stories and suggestions for improvement at *Peter@gamsatreview.com*

CREDITS

The chapter on Multiple Mini Interviews was written by Pita Rahm ex faculty member in the English department and Director of Quality Assurance at the University of Belize. Pita was also seconded to the Ministry of Health for one year to manage a multi-million dollar health sector reform project.

.

Printed in Great Britain
by Amazon.co.uk, Ltd.,
Marston Gate.